YO-CBG-742

#1 *NEW YORK TIMES* BESTSELLING AUTHOR

MIKE EVANS

LIVING FEAR
FREE

TIMEWORTHY
BOOKS

P.O. Box 30000, Phoenix, AZ 85046

TABLE OF CONTENTS

CHAPTER ONE

Looking For Acceptance

So many Believers are too intimidated to show their
true emotions for fear of condemnation. The hurt,
guilt and shame are too real, which causes people to
run from their pain. God does not want you to live as
a captive to fear and rejection! There is a remedy.

Today's average Americans find themselves overwhelmed and anxious in a world of economic and political uncertainty. With a collapsed economy, corporate banks that are going bankrupt, a mortgage meltdown, a housing crash, Wall Street and auto industry bailouts, high unemployment, and a deflated dollar, many wonder where our nation is headed. Every day, we see global media outlets unveiling the turbulence in the Middle East. Conflicts with Israel and her neighboring enemies, riots in Syria, and a clash over the Suez Canal are causing oil prices to skyrocket. We see those things, not to mention international trepidation because Iran is intent on manufacturing a nuclear weapon. Nations, fearing a potential World War III, are stricken with apprehension!

I do not have to convince you that fear is predominate in the world today; but what I do have to convince you is that there is a *remedy* for fear. When addressing the topic of fear, I realize there are multiple factors and reasons why it overpowers individuals, and in this book, *Living Fear Free*, I will address many of them in forthcoming chapters.

First, you must understand that fear is a spirit. The origin behind fear is a spiritual force that attacks the inner you—your soul, which results in a fierce battle raging in your mind, emotions and will, destroying your potential dreams, and if not dealt with properly, eventually robbing you of your destiny. Once a spirit of fear takes root, you lose control of your emotions, sending you spiraling downward into a spiritual pit of despair, discouragement and disappointment.

This condition opens the door to a number of vulnerabilities, weaknesses and misconceptions. Immediately, you become a victim to F.E.A.R. (False Evidence Appearing Real). One of those false evidences appearing real is rejection. When you develop a spirit of fear, rejection follows. Then, the need for acceptance, recognition and approval motivates your actions and dictates your behavior. When you do not feel accepted, suddenly you feel *rejected* by God and by others.

When it comes to daily life, rejection can cause you to misread and misinterpret events, people, and even God. Right away, you become paranoid, suspicious and mistrusting, clouding the decision-making process, and it usually leads to terrible mistakes. The fear of rejection also creates a tendency to put up walls, shut people out, question God and His Word, and to try to find ways to prevent humiliation. Trapped in a world of fear, rejection leads you to assume "something" that simply is not true. Faulty perceptions overpower reason, and before you know it, you are a mess.

Jacob, of the Bible, is a person of interest when it comes to rejection. He too suffered with this problem and it caused him to succumb to faulty assumptions and make unwise decisions that were life-altering. For illustrative purposes, I would like to use Jacob as an example as one who struggled with the spirit of fear and rejection, but eventually conquered both of them.

Family Feud

Jacob and Esau were twins; Jacob was the younger of the two boys. Trapped in a family feud of favoritism, their father, Isaac, loved Esau, but Rebekah, their mother, loved Jacob (Genesis 25:28). Despite Jacob's reservations and fear of coming under a curse, the maternal preferential treatment from his mother and her overbearing personality led Jacob to succumb to a deceptive plan that would trick his aging, blind father into passing on the birthright that was intended for Esau.

Esau's absence on a hunting trip provided a perfect opportunity for Rebekah to aid Jacob in despicable plot to conceal his physical features and present himself as his twin brother. Her intent was to swindle Esau's birthright as the firstborn from Isaac. The strategy worked, but once Isaac discovered what Jacob had done, he shook with immense despair, and Esau burned in anger, ready to take vengeance on Jacob for his dishonest actions.

Thus, Jacob feared for his life and the hostile atmosphere forced Isaac to ban Jacob from their dwelling, sending his youngest son out as a sojourner. Even though Jacob loved his father, and submitted to the authority of his mother, he was rejected and sent away in shame (Genesis 27:45).

Fear and rejection will destroy you. Sometimes it starts when you are a child. When I was a boy, I developed a poor self-image of myself because of a broken relationship with my father. I was fearful and, in my mind, believed I had been rejected. But that was not *God's* image of me!

Like Jacob, I struggled with my identity when I was young. I was very shy and withdrawn, and when in public, wouldn't look at anyone. When somebody came to the door, I ran and hid. I developed a stuttering problem. People laughed at me, so I decided not to talk. I ended up quitting school and leaving home. Since I was underage, I tricked my father into signing the appropriate papers so I could join the army.

Rejected people usually try to find the path of least resistance. I was anxious, worried, and hurting. I thought the only way to survive was to avoid people. By choosing that route, no one would know my name, no one would call on me, and I would not be required to respond. In other words, I would not be rejected again. A spirit of rejection kept me from dealing with my circumstances and caused me to make unwise decisions!

A Way in the Wilderness

Jacob was forced into the wilderness...alone and on the run. He traveled east to a faraway land and became a sheep herder. There, Jacob met Rachael whom he desired as his wife. After meeting the ancient Near East custom requirements for marriage, Jacob's future father-in-law, Laban, defrauded him by giving Jacob his elder daughter, Leah, instead. Over time, Jacob had a family, but he always looked over his shoulder, waiting for Esau to take revenge.

Eventually, his brother Esau and their contentious past confronted Jacob. As he watched his brother approach, Jacob wanted to flee, because he thought Esau was going to kill him. Instead, Jacob sent one of his wives and his children ahead to appease his brother. He was willing to sacrifice his family to save himself. However, Esau was not planning to hurt him, but that's what Jacob thought, because of a spirit of rejection.

Nevertheless, conditions changed over time, and it softened Esau's heart. When he finally faced Jacob after all those years, he forgave him (Genesis 33:4). Their broken relationship was healed, the past forgotten and the spirit of rejection reversed.

Rehearse, Re-curse or Reverse

If you are like most people, you want to feel secure, to respect yourself, and to know you are loved. Unfortunately, none of these desires will be realized if a spirit of rejection controls you. However, three options are available to you:

1. You can *rehearse* all the dreadful things that have happened to you and develop a bad attitude toward life. A bad attitude will kill you. Zig Ziglar said, "It is attitude, not aptitude, which determines altitude.[1]

   How far you go with God will be determined by your attitude. You have either an attitude of trust, or a fearful attitude that causes you to mistrust everyone.

   Repeatedly, Jacob rehearsed how he had hurt his brother, and he anticipated how he was going to be killed for it. When you rehearse the past, you live your life as a living "dead" person, complaining about everything because you feel rejected.

2. You can *re-curse* and vow to "get even" with those that wronged you, which leads to bitterness. Bitterness causes you to lash out at everyone around you with your words and attitude.

   You can spend your whole life cursing your past. It's like cursing a fruit tree. You may not like the fruit you see, but if you curse it, you deny yourself the nourishment that tree could give you. Another problem is that death often follows curses, and if your "fruit tree" dies, then you have lost even the possibility of eating the fruit that tree could have provided.

3. You can *reverse* the past. Everybody loses when a person is captive to a spirit of rejection. Do you know someone who seems to be miserable most of the time? More than likely, that individual still feels wounded from the past.

Christians often pretend that everything is alright when, in fact, their lives are full of chaos. Many Believers are afraid to show their true emotions because they think it would be ungodly. They do not want to be hurt, but God does not want us to live as captives to fear and rejection. He wants us to *reverse* our situation!

Jacob had plenty of reasons to feel rejected, but despite his actions, God continuously pursued him to reassure Jacob he was loved. On several occasions, God showed up reaffirming that He had a plan for Jacob. This is what God had to say about him:

"But now thus saith the Lord that created thee, O Jacob, and he that formed thee, O Israel, Fear not: for I have redeemed thee, I have called thee by thy name; and thou art mine. When thou passest through the waters, I will be with thee; and through the rivers, they shall not overflow thee: when thou walkest through the fire, thou shalt not be burned; neither shall the flame kindle upon thee" (Isaiah 43:1-2).

I'm Not Good Enough

I remember on one occasion, when I paid a compliment to a young lady, telling her that the dress she was wearing was very pretty.

She said, "This old thing? It's too long and my necklace doesn't even match my dress."

She wouldn't let me pay her a compliment.

No matter what you do or say, you cannot bless these types of people because they are always suspicious, thinking that you have an ulterior motive, or that you are insincere. By rejecting a blessing, they are letting you know they are hurting. They are saying, "I'm not good enough." For many people, it is too frightening to let God touch them where they hurt and bring healing. They would rather play the "Blame Game." For some reason, people tend to blend guilt with blame. When you are bound, people do not admit anything. Instead, they criticize others.

Christians often are trapped in this same cycle. Why? Because they are hurting, and they don't receive the Word of the Lord. Instead, they listen to the criticism they hear. They focus on their failures. They view their life as a mess and the world as a mess. Hope is not an option. They only see the bad things that are happening. They are rehearsing their hurts, their circumstances, and the people around them.

Declare a Thing

How does a Christian begin to *reverse* his or her situation? The answer is found in the book of Job. God's promises and decrees are important for His people. In fact, they are vital! God asked Job, "What is the deal? Why have you been rehearsing and re-cursing?" The Lord told Job to stop and *decree* "a thing." When you decree what *God* says is true about your life, then it will be established.

"Thou shalt also decree a thing, and it shall be established unto thee: and the light shall shine upon thy ways. When men are cast down, then thou shalt say, there is lifting up; and he shall save the humble person. He shall deliver the island of the innocent: and it is delivered by the pureness of thine hands" (Job 22:28-30).

When we repeat what God says, we can reverse the curse! So, why don't Christians do this more often? Mainly because they listen to the devil, the ex-employee of God, who was fired and then kicked off the premises.

God was telling Job, "Not only will you decree My promises for your life, but I will take you into a new dimension of living. Then you will take downcast men and decree something, and *they* will be lifted up."

What that literally means is that by your efforts, you will deliver individuals who are in sin, rebellion, and disobedience. God is giving you a promise for your children, your family, and your friends. They may be in sin, but God will deliver them by the pureness of your hands if you will *decree* God's promises.

Living with Turkeys

Let me tell you the story of two eagles. We will call "Jan" and "Sam." They were baby eaglets, so their mother always came to feed them; however, one day, the mother disappeared, and Jan and Sam became very hungry. So, they decided to do something about it. Nestled high up on the cliffs, they jumped out of their nest. With no flying experience, they panicked, flapped their wings like crazy, soared out of control, and hit the ground.

Jan and Sam survived the fall and landed in a field of turkeys. Startled with their arrival, the turkeys were troubled. They came to Jan and Sam and asked, "Who are you?" However, Jan and Sam didn't know who or what they were.

So they asked the turkeys, "What are we?"

The turkeys paused and said, "You are turkeys." Since Jan and Sam did not walk or talk like turkeys, it was decided that they needed to have special training. The training began, but they could not do anything right.

The turkeys fed Jan and Sam acorns, but it made them ill. One day, Sam became rebellious over the food selection. The turkey boss said, "You had better stop acting like that, or everyone will find out what you really are. You are just a buzzard, and everyone hates buzzards." That offended Sam, so he took off to find some turkeys that were more like him. Sometime later, Sam found some turkeys that ate berries, so he settled with them. He discovered that berries were tasty, but not filling.

One day, while feeding, Sam stretched and flapped his wings, which caused him to elevate off the ground. Amazed, he discovered that he could fly. Soaring high in the air, he could see everything below. When lifted above his circumstances, above the turkeys and the turkey training, Sam saw something new. He realized there was a whole world he had never seen before; but his fear of heights caused him to return to the ground and resume his life as a turkey.

A few days later, Sam was talking with an old owl. The owl said, "You look like you're starving."

Sam replied, "I am. I have been eating berries and acorns. The berries don't satisfy my hunger, and the acorns make me sick." The owl questioned him as to why he was doing that.

He answered, "Because I am a turkey, and that is what turkeys eat."

The owl said, "Hate to tell ya, but you're not a turkey."

That upset Sam so much, he ran away from the old owl, because he thought the owl was going to call him a buzzard.

You Are an Eagle

Many Christians are like Sam. A spirit of rejection binds them, and they refuse to pursue freedom because they are afraid someone will call them something worse than a turkey. They think they know what dismal creatures they are, and they are afraid somebody else will find out

As Sam ran off, the owl yelled, "Relax... You're not a turkey, Sam. You're the finest ... most loyal and honorable bird of all. You're a beautiful eagle!" But Sam did not hear it because he ran.

The spirit of rejection will cause you to run away from truth. The wisdom of the old owl could have set Sam free, but he had lived a life as a turkey for so long, he couldn't see himself any other way. Instead, he remained defeated.

Three things will defeat you when you are subscribing to the spirit of rejection:

1. Committing to negative *emotions*. These will take away the

strength God gives to overcome rejection.

2.   Committing to negative *people*. Negative people will sap your energy and suck the life out of you.

3.   Committing to a negative *atmosphere*. Listening to negative words and songs, watching negative shows on television and reading negative books deprive you of the truth and encouragement you really need. It is like eating nothing but junk food all day, every day. You feel "filled up,'" but you are full of empty thoughts!

Let God do a new thing in your life. Isaiah said it like this: *"Don't remember the former things. Behold, I do something new!"* (43:19).

Preventing Rejection

To avoid internalizing your painful experiences of rejection, you must proactively make a choice to face your fears. If you are struggling with rejection because of a divorce, childhood abuse/neglect, discrimination, repeated failures, or any other acts of betrayal you need to convey your feelings and experiences to the Lord, and in some cases, to a pastor or a Christian counselor, no matter how shameful or painful it may be. In doing so, you reduce your feeling of aloneness. As you face your fears, and share the emotions provoked by your experience, you are sure to encounter others with similar stories . . . maybe worse. This is very vital in "turning the tide" of being rejected. Suddenly, your focus shifts from you, and what you may, or may not have done, to the knowledge that rejection is just an experience like any other negative experience. There is a remedy.

Rejection is never easy, but rejection from people we care about really hurts. Maybe it's the rejection of losing your job or having a spouse walk out on you. Sometimes rejection can be so devastating we are not sure we are going to recover. The devil will try to destroy a child of God with rejection by using deception and distraction.

There are 5 ways you can prevent rejection from gaining a stronghold in your life:

1. *Jesus understands.* On the cross, He faced the rejection of the whole world. Be honest with God about your feelings. He understands.

2. *Don't seek revenge.* Trust God to bring about ultimate justice. Ask God to help you forgive. After all, Jesus forgave us for rejecting Him on the cross.

3. *Develop a Conquering Mentality.* Filling your mind with God's Word will develop positive thoughts, causing you to see things from His perspective.

4. *Don't confuse forgiveness with a lack of accountability.* Holding wrongdoers accountable is good—for them, for us, and for others.

5. *Choose to get better, not bitter.* The best way to get even in a good way is to get better. Remember, "Bitterness is the poison we swallow while hoping the other person dies."

By implementing these 5 preventive life-applications for rejection, you can take authority over the spirit of fear and rejection, and decree God's Word in your life.

Life is not for the weak, but for the strong in God! There will be battles, but they provide opportunities to grow. A battle is often seen as opposition, but the truth is that it is an essential part of the journey. You may be in a major battle, but you are on the road to a miracle! No one alive today ever experienced a miracle or a great victory in his life without going through battles. Struggle is proof that you have not been left alone. If you are still fighting, at least you know you have not been beaten!

Say what God says, and move from rejection to God's acceptance! Knowing that God loves you and accepts you can change everything. If you are *looking for acceptance*, find it in God first, and then He will heal your wounds and break the spirit of fear and rejection, and restore what has been lost.

CHAPTER TWO

See with the Kingdom Eyes

As a Believer, we must never forget that even in our
darkest times, God is at work and He has a plan.

For a Christian, truth is not in the eye of the beholder but is based on the Word of God. However, our perception of what is happening in our life can affect our faith—and determine how we will respond. When it comes to life's challenges, people often ask, "What's happening?" or "What's going on?" There is a difference between what we see and what is really happening. Many Christians are simply afraid to face reality, so they rely on their interpretation of the facts. But as a child of God, we are called to walk in truth and light.

A good example of perception versus truth is found in the book of Daniel. After spending nearly seventy years in captivity, away from their homeland, the people of Israel had their perception of things, but God revealed a deeper reality to Daniel. When faced with calamity or confusion, it is easy to look at things from experience and miss the big picture. As a Believer, we must never forget that even in our darkest times, God is at work and He has a plan. We might not always perceive it, but reality is not always what we see.

Son of David

A prime example of the conflict between perception and reality is found in the gospels. The story of Bartimaeus involves a blind beggar and it is the last of the healing miracles recorded by Mark:

"And they came to Jericho: and as he went out of Jericho with his disciples and a great number of people, blind Bartimaeus, the son of Timaeus, sat by the highway side begging. And when he heard that it was Jesus of Nazareth, he began to cry out, and say, Jesus, thou son of David, have mercy on me" (Mark 10:46, 47).

This man made an unusual pronouncement declaring that Jesus was the "Son of David." In other words, Bartimaeus acknowledged that Jesus was and *is* the kingly Messiah through his lineage with David. Isn't it amazing that the man who was blind could see who He was, but those who were experts of the Law and Scriptures could not see Jesus as the Son of David?

A Garment of Bondage

Not everyone agreed with his remarks:

"Many charged him that he should hold his peace: but he cried the more a great deal, Thou son of David, have mercy on me. And Jesus stood still, and commanded him to be called. And they called the blind man, saying unto him, Be of good comfort, rise; he calleth thee. And he, casting away his garment, rose, and came to Jesus" (Mark 10:48-50).

Bartimaeus was a beggar. There were three common areas where beggars could be found: at the gate of the temple, at holy rivers or springs, and on the highway or public thoroughfare. Historians tell us beggars carried a garment that identified a person's condition, which qualified one for pleading for financial assistance or would tell what type of ailment or disease they might carry. Depending upon the handicap, the article of clothing would depict what type of beggar he was. In this case, Bartimaeus was blind; thus, he could not wear ordinary clothing.

In addition, blind people were not allowed to remove their garment unless they no longer were handicapped or diseased. And the longer they wore the garment, the more it became a stronghold of bondage in their lives.

Cast It Off

To outsiders, Bartimaeus' garment showed he was a man without the blessings of God. And the reaction to his cry affirmed their position as they attempted to silence him. But the Bible says the blind man cast off his garment, not *after* he was healed, but *before*. He cast it off to *be* healed. This was an important act of faith. In order to live free of fear and what others think about you, you must be willing to cast off what labels you.

Do not look at what's going on around you. Do not develop an attitude that is limited by the here and now. Commit yourself to a God who knows what is really happening in your life and cast off your blind man's garment. Bartimaeus cast off his garment when he heard the word from Jesus. He experienced the reality of the song, "Every stronghold of bondage will fall at my feet."

Cast off the lies that prevent you from seeing the truth about yourself, as revealed in God's Word. The mercy of God is far greater than your sin or your own inaccurate self-image. You can learn from your past, as I have. Let God show you the truth about your past, and His purpose for you in each circumstance.

The abuse I suffered, the rejection I felt, the fear and low self-esteem could have scarred me for the rest of my life. Instead, I have chosen to look at life with "kingdom eyes" and see Jesus through it all!

Acknowledge Your Need

Who was Bartimaeus anyway? He was a homeless man with nothing to live for, just like the homeless people you may see on the streets today. Can you imagine the scene that Mark described long ago? Something happened to the blind man. In the midst of all the shouting and despite the heat and dust, the blind man heard a noise. Anything, a cart tipping over, or people bartering over the price of oranges could have caused the noise. But that was not what was happening.

Bartimaeus could have lost the miracle of his healing if he had been concerned with what others thought of him. Notice, Jesus did not go to him—Bartimaeus had to call out to Jesus. Not just once, but repeatedly, before he got a response. He had to persist, despite the crowd's warning that he had better be quiet. Bartimaeus could have said, "If I am supposed to be healed, then Jesus will come to me. If He is the Messiah, then He will notice me." But that's not what happened. If he had focused on his circumstances, it would have destroyed his faith. Bartimaeus was helpless, not hopeless!

The Bible says that he was in *desperate need*. When you have a need, it is time to take action. Don't let a miracle pass you by when you need it, stand up and cast off what is hindering you and cry out to God!

Look Toward Heaven

Bartimaeus did not let his blindness dictate what he "saw." He turned his eyes toward heaven. He was looking for a miracle. If your eyes are accustomed to the darkness, it is natural that you will expect to see darkness wherever you try to look. When you look with faith, blind eyes are opened.

As Bartimaeus began to cry out, other people reprimanded him, trying to silence his voice. The religious leaders scornfully rebuked him. They probably wanted to test Jesus to see if He could *prove* He was really the Messiah. They wanted to see Him *perform*, but they did not believe He was really the King of kings and Lord of lords. Bartimaeus was willing to be humiliated and scolded by the entire town if that meant Jesus would stop and meet him at his point of need.

In the midst of your need today, whether it is a financial need, a physical healing, emotional restoration, or a miracle in your home, the devil will say to you, "Shut up! God will not hear you. Can't you see what is going on? Jesus is too busy. He doesn't care about you." *Don't be fooled by the lies of the devil!* Bartimaeus said, "Have mercy on me." In essence, he was saying, "Jesus, I am not focusing on what's going on around me, but focusing on You."

Kingdom Eyes Are Better

If you read the Book of Hebrews, you will see one word more than any other, "better". Hebrews says you are a *better* person than the high priest, a *better* covenant, a *better* sacrifice, a *better* promise. God's grace and mercy were not based upon Bartimaeus' condition, nor were they based upon his sin. Jesus responded in grace and mercy when Bartimaeus cast off his garment and presented his need to the Lord. *Bartimaeus touched the heart of God and God touched the life of Bartimaeus.*

The grace of God enables you to receive and empowers you to live as He desires you to live. Many people have the mistaken idea that "God hates sinners and loves the righteous." Yet, exactly the opposite is true. God loves sinners and despises self-righteousness. When men pronounce defeat, Jesus pronounces victory. This happens only when you can see through "kingdom eyes."

The Bible relates that when the Hebrew baby boys in Egypt had been given the death sentence. A mother knew that her little baby, Moses, was also doomed to die. But she had a promise from God. Instead of letting fear paralyze her, she looked at her circumstances from God's perspective. She laid her baby in a basket and set it adrift in the Nile. It must have been difficult to watch her son float away in the river in a manmade "boat", but somehow she believed he would be safe. He was, after all, in God's hands.

That baby was Moses who would grow up to become the deliverer who led Israel out of Egyptian bondage. Through Moses' leadership, the people of Israel witnessed glorious miracles repeatedly. His faithfulness sparked the faith of men like Caleb and Joshua, who eventually led the Israelites into the Promised Land. An entire nation was changed because one woman dared to look beyond her circumstances and see with *kingdom eyes*.

When the angel Gabriel came to Mary and declared that she would become pregnant with the Son of God, she said, *"Be it unto me according to thy Word."* Others probably said, "We know what is going on here, Mary. You are an immoral woman. You should be stoned to death." They did not see with *kingdom eyes*.

When King Herod heard that the King of kings had been born he tried to kill all the Jewish baby boys, age two and under. Herod was threatened by the birth of Jesus. He too did not see with *kingdom eyes*, and because of his fear, many innocent children were murdered.

God Is Faithful

The book of Esther tells about Haman, a man who wanted to kill all the Jews. He plotted a plan of destruction through deceit and lies, and convinced the king to build gallows built for Mordecai and his family. He said, "The Jews are a growing nuisance. If I can kill Mordecai, I can kill the entire Jewish population, and my problem will be solved." He was convinced his plan would permit him to *see* that Mordecai would hang on the gallows.

What Haman did not know was that Queen Esther was a Jewish

woman who knew how to see with *kingdom eyes*. Despite her initial fears, she interceded on Mordecai's behalf and his life was spared. As for Haman, well, he died on the gallows he had built for Mordecai! The Jews were delivered; once again, because one woman dared to look past her circumstances and dared to set aside her personal comfort and safety. She dared to believe the Word and the promise of God. *"And who knoweth whether thou art come to the kingdom for such a time as this."* (Esther 4:14). From *God's* perspective, He had a plan even while the gallows were being built.

The Bible says David lived in the city of Ziklag, the city of despair. He was anointed to be king. Although he had killed the giant, Goliath, he still lived as a defeated man in the midst of his enemies. The Philistines stole everything David had, including his children and his wife. When everything looked bad, David encouraged himself in the Lord. He looked beyond his circumstances and saw God's faithfulness.

When you look at Jesus on the cross, you see two thieves beside Him. You see a man who was beaten and abandoned. You see the precious Savior, naked, humiliated, and scorned. Jesus had the power to call angels to stop the crucifixion. But He didn't. Why? Because He knew how to see with *Kingdom eyes*. He sacrificed His life and ministry, everything He had, so you could *know* Him as the Truth. His definition of reality goes beyond mere circumstances; it is based on faith in a loving God who orders your steps and directs your path.

Salvation Settled—Once for All

That day was a turning point for the entire world. The men and women who witnessed the brutality of the scourging and the horror of the crucifixion thought Jesus' life was finished. But it wasn't. Jesus' work was finished but not His plan. His life pointed to the cross, to His victory over sin, death, and hell. His loving sacrifice and His glorious resurrection guaranteed that our salvation is settled once and

Small t truth or Capital T truth.

for all.

Where are you today? Are you living in fear and defeat because of your circumstances? Or, are you looking past those circumstances to see with *Kingdom eyes*? What is God saying through your circumstances? Here are three simple steps to follow when you think all is lost and there is no way out:

1. *Acknowledge God as your source.* If Bartimaeus had made anything other than God his source, he would have become bitter and barren. He wouldn't have had his need met. The first thing the devil will do when you are in need is make a list of everyone who could help you but won't. God is your source!

2. *Maintain your joy.* Bartimaeus had plenty of reasons not to have joy, but he trusted the Lord and found abundant joy and new vision.

3. *Keep looking toward heaven.* If Bartimaeus had become distracted by everything that was going on around him, he would never have received his miracle. But his eyes were turned heavenward. Something in his spirit moved him and he focused his attention on heaven. He saw his situation from God's perspective and there he received hope and healing.

The Bible says, *"Jesus answered and said unto him, What wilt thou that I should do unto thee? The blind man said unto him, Lord, that I might receive my sight. And Jesus said unto him, Go thy way; thy faith hath made thee whole. And immediately he received his sight, and followed Jesus in the way."* (Mark 10:51, 52) *"In the way"* implies that he became a disciple of Jesus Christ. He was more than grateful for this act of mercy, he went one step further, and he actually submitted his life to the Lordship of Jesus.

When you see things with kingdom eyes, you must act upon it with faith. Do not hold back. Do not let fear dictate your future. Pursue God and follow Him all the way!

CHAPTER THREE

Deal with the Real

Life in Jesus and in His Word is the only reality—
everything else is superficial.

To be used by God, your priorities must be focused more on the spirit realm than the natural realm. Life in Jesus and in His Word is the only reality—everything else is superficial. The Bible says, "*Then spake the Lord to Paul in the night by a vision, Be not afraid, but speak, and hold not thy peace.*" (Acts 18:9) What do words have to do with faith—and fear? God told Paul, "Don't have fear, but speak," as though *speaking* would disarm the fear.

When people are fearful, they tend to speak according to what they see. When overwhelmed by circumstances, many focus on the negative and thereby lose their hope. Fear, like faith, grows according to your words. If you speak out of fear, you will become more fearful. If, however, you confess your faith in God, *despite* your circumstances, you will be encouraged and you will find your faith stronger than ever. After all, what you need is stronger faith and less fear, isn't it? God wants us to deal with the real—life in Jesus that transforms us into people of the kingdom—not with surface realities.

A Thousand Needles

When my son, Michael, was just a boy, he ran into the house one day, upset and overcome with fear based upon a fabricated threat from his sister. "Rachie said she was going to stick a thousand needles in my eye!" he cried.

I said, "Son, you will never see the day that happens."

"You better believe it," he answered, "because when there are a thousand needles in my eye, I won't be seeing at all!"

Some people live as though they have a thousand needles in their eye. They hear about kingdom reality, but they really do not believe it works. They do not see God's reality in their own lives, so they make excuses. They let fear keep them from living by faith. What about you? Do you dismiss people who are doing great things for God because you do not see His reality in your life?

You are no less important to God than your pastor, or any other leader in the Church. St. Augustine said, "God loves each one of us as if there was only one of us to love."[1] God has called *you* to do great things in Jesus' name, but you won't fulfill that calling unless you get *into faith* and *out of fear.*

Living in fear is like living near a poisoned stream. If you drink from it, for the moment it will quench your thirst, but the result is death. Some people think fear is an effective motivator, but fear doesn't motivate anyone to grow, spiritually or otherwise. It only leads to deeper deception and greater bondage.

Throughout your life, you will deal constantly with two spirits—faith and fear. With faith comes power and with fear comes paralysis. The Bible describes many individuals who were conquerors in life. They fulfilled their destiny and influenced the world because they spoke the truth—God's truth— and were not afraid.

What do the words of your mouth reveal about you? Do they reflect your faith in God, or do they indicate your bondage to fear?

A Light in Your Face

King David is a great example of a man who knew how to speak the Word and disarm fear. When confronted by a menacing giant named Goliath, he said, *"The Lord is my light and my salvation. Whom shall I fear?"* Like David, when confronted by giants in your own life, remember what David said, *"The Lord is my light and my salvation. Whom shall I fear?"*

The Bible tells us that David *hid in a cave* as war raged about him and his foes pursued him relentlessly. But David took words from God and used them as weapons to conquer his fear! He overcame both his fear and his foes, and God *blessed* his faith!

Look at Paul. He faced many crises in his life. People verbally attacked him and some even tried to kill him. Yet, he was not afraid. Why? Because he had confidence in God.

Have you ever read one of those self-help books written to build confidence? I have. I have read many of them over the years. But, they did me no good. I could not relate to those authors. They talked about developing self-confidence, but confidence in *self* is not what I needed. The Bible does not talk about self-confidence; it says you should put your confidence in God!

God's Anointing

I have been asked many times, "How do you minister to world leaders?" Well, it is not because I am smart. I simply have an anointing. I go in and speak to them without intimidation because the Spirit of God is upon me, and He puts the words in my mouth.

God is the one who gives you favor with men and governments. In my travels, I have met people of all races, in various levels of importance, from numerous lifestyles who want to know one thing: how can an individual overcome fear? The Holy Spirit gives you opportu-

Isaiah 50:4 The Lord has given me an instructed
Sovereign
tongue, to know the word to sustain the weary.

23

nities to speak the truth in love and, with each opportunity He will give you the anointing you need to speak. He gives you the *wisdom* and the *words* that will minister life—but you must be willing to listen and obey.

You know, in the natural, Paul should have been on a major guilt trip. He had persecuted the Church. He had *killed* Christians. Why, then, did Paul become so dynamic? Why was he able to conquer fear and impact the world with his teachings? What is the difference between Paul and you? He just had a whole lot of Jesus, and he understood the importance of speaking the truth.

Paul saw reality from God's perspective, and he let that reality permeate every part of his life. He accepted whatever God said as truth, whether it was about himself, the Church, the Jews, or the Gentiles.

We live in a world that is full of excuses. If you ask someone why they do not believe in the Word, they will tell you, "I am disappointed in so-and-so." But let me tell you—Paul didn't put his trust in man; he put his faith in God.

Sixty-six Reasons for Success

I can give you sixty-six reasons why you will succeed if you start speaking the Word of God—the sixty-six books of the Bible! What will you get from God without faith? Nothing. What are you doing about all your problems? Worrying? Is it helping? Of course not. Will complaining help? Not a chance.

Why don't you start speaking the Word of God into your situation? Write the Scriptures down and start confessing them. Reverse the curse by speaking the Word.

You must learn to *deal with the real.* If you have fear, deal with it. If God has given you an assignment, no matter what it is, do not quit. You cannot lose if you do not quit!

It does not matter how many reversals you have; if you cannot be stopped you will ultimately succeed. What keeps people from success is their deterioration from faith into fear. So many people give up for silly reasons. They give up on their jobs, marriages, schools, children, churches, and even God. Why? Because of fear.

Jesus had the toughest assignment in the world, yet He never offered an excuse. He never said, "I just can't do this, God." Nothing and no one could keep Jesus from doing what He had been called to do. Jesus said, *"What the Father says, I say. What the Father does, I do. If you have seen My Father, then you have seen Me."* Jesus set an example for us.

Get Desperate

You may have heard of Joni Eareckson Tada who was once a champion diver. On a summer day in 1967, she dove into the Chesapeake Bay after misjudging the shallowness of the water and suffered a severe injury that paralyzed her from the neck down. From a natural point of view, she is severely limited. What can she do when she can't move a finger, an arm, or a leg?

Joni, a beautiful woman, got into the Word of God and started *speaking* the Word. She stopped feeling sorry for herself and blaming others and as a result, she has touched thousands of lives. She learned to paint beautiful pictures by holding a paintbrush in *her mouth. She* has written over 40 books, recorded several music albums, starred in an autobiographical movie of her life, earned seven honorary Doctorates, and won numerous awards.[2]

Nothing seems to hold Joni back. She does more than most women who are whole. Why? Because she was desperate enough to believe and act upon the Word of God and be filled with His power.

Whoever would have thought Franklin D. Roosevelt could become President of the United States while he was confined to a wheelchair? Whoever dreamed that Napoleon, an epileptic who suffered from frequent seizures, could conquer a continent?

Walt Disney dared to show his little cartoon to some business people and asked them to help finance his vision for animated film. They thought his idea was stupid. "You're not an artist," they told him. "Besides, no one is going to want to see a story about a mouse; people don't even like mice!" But now the whole world knows Walt Disney and his creation: Mickey Mouse.

Whoever would have thought that Beethoven, who became totally deaf, could continue to write beautiful music?

Catch His Vision

God is asking you today, "What do you want to do with your life?" Get the vision *He* wants to give you and do not be afraid! Deal with your fear and allow Him to guide you each step of the way.

Years ago, I spent the day with some dear friends, Jim and Jeanne Rogers. Jeanne has a dynamic ministry as a singer and praise leader. She has sung at conferences across the nation, taught music workshops, and appeared on television. But as a young woman, Jeanne felt the pain of rejection. Her mother was divorced two or three times and her father, an alcoholic, abandoned her when she was a baby. But today, people look at her and say, "What a marvelous lady and a wonderful singer!"

Look at Evangelist James Robison. When he was born, his mother put an ad in the newspaper asking for someone to raise him. A godly pastor and his wife took James into their home as a foster child and shared the love of God with him.

But the promise of a loving family didn't last. Throughout his childhood, James was shuffled between the foster home where he felt safe and the house where his mother lived. There, he faced poverty, rejection, and abuse by an alcoholic father.

Today, James Robison is one of the most dynamic evangelists anywhere. His organization, LIFE Outreach International, is bringing the life and love of Jesus to sick, starving, forgotten people all across the globe. In southern Africa alone, LIFE Outreach is helping to feed more than 60,000 children every month—and seeing multitudes saved through the power of the gospel.

What happened to these people? By God's grace, they stopped feeling sorry for themselves. They faced their fear and put their faith in Jesus. They saw reality from God's perspective and allowed it to redefine their future. They believed He had His hand on their lives, and they trusted Him—no matter what their circumstances told them.

Stop making excuses. Being angry at the world for your misfortunes will get you nowhere. You need to say, "God, You have a plan for my life. Show me that plan, and help me fulfill the call You have on my life. I trust You, and I thank You for loving me."

CHAPTER FOUR

Develop Mountain-Moving Faith

*God wants to deliver you from fear and lead you into
a life of uncompromising faith.*

D
wight L. Moody once said, "Faith that fizzles in the finish
has a flaw in the beginning." For many Christians, faith is
a concept, not a reality. It is easier for them to *talk* about
faith than to *walk* by it, but the Bible says it is impossible to please
God without faith. What kind of faith pleases the Lord? Faith that
can be tested and can be stretched ...mountain-moving faith! *"And
Jesus answering saith unto them, Have faith in God. For verily I say
unto you, That whosoever shall say unto this IL mountain, Be thou removed and be thou cast into the sea; and shall not doubt in his heart,
but shall believe that those things which he saith shall come to pass; he
shall have whatsoever he saith."* (Mark 11:22-23).

To survive in today's world, you need faith—but the right kind of
faith. Not flawed faith that "fizzles in the end." That isn't really faith
at all, is it? Hebrews 11:1 says, *"Now faith is the assurance (the confirmation, the title deed) of the things we hope for, being the proof of things
we do not see and the conviction of their reality—faith perceiving as*

real fact what is not revealed to the senses." (Amplified)

Many Christians struggle with fear because they do not possess the kind of faith that moves mountains. In fact, they do not have molehill moving faith! They rely more on their *emotions* to guide them through tough times rather than relying on the Word of God. Emotions are tied to our senses and we use them every day.

When you got up this morning, you had to utilize your senses, didn't you? Perhaps you heard the sound of an alarm clock, telling you it was time to wake up. Then, you looked at the clock, just to make sure. You got out of bed, took a shower, and put on your clothes. You felt the water, then the texture of clothing against your skin. As you walked into the kitchen, you smelled the aroma of fresh-brewed coffee. You tasted it and felt its heat. All of your senses work together to help you process information about your surroundings. They enable you to assess your environment and make judgments about it.

There are productive individuals who survive without one or two of their senses—hearing or sight, for instance—but unless a person uses all the senses he has, he will not be able to function in the natural world.

But, this is not true in the spiritual realm. Although you need your five senses to assess your natural surroundings, you cannot rely on them when you are making spiritual judgments. If you do, you could be misled by physical information that has little or nothing to do with spiritual reality. That's where faith comes in.

A Measure of Faith

If you want to sharpen your senses, you must give yourself opportunities to develop them. Perfumers, for example, spend years perfecting their sense of smell. After diligent practice, they can identify all sorts of scents and tell whether they are floral or woodsy, oriental or grassy. They can analyze a fragrance and determine if it has jasmine or rose oil in it. They know if it has lilac. Some can even identify which scents are synthetic. Really good perfumers are actually called "noses"!

Romans 12:3 says, *"...God hath dealt to every man the measure of faith."* You have received a measure of faith! If you want to develop your faith, you have to exercise it. What does that mean? *"So then faith cometh by hearing, and hearing by the word of God."* (Romans 10:17). Can you develop your faith simply by going to church and listening to good preaching? Yes, you can increase your faith that way. But, relying solely on your sense of hearing will not turn your faith into mountain-moving faith. You must *hear* the Word of God with your heart!

Hearing the Word of God is not the same as listening to it. *Hearing* goes beyond the physical act. It engages the heart—and it begins, not with the ear, but with the eye. If you want to develop mountain-moving faith, you must be in the Word every day. You must read it and let God speak to you through it. From there, you begin to latch onto truths that impact you, and you step out in faith.

Speaking the Word

Mountain-moving faith is developed over time and to increase your faith you must *practice* by confessing God's truth with your mouth. When you are faced with a crisis, speak the Word! If you are wrestling with fear, diffuse it with the Word. *"For God hath not given us the spirit of fear; but of power, and of love, arid of a sound mind."* (2 Timothy 1:7).

The devil attacks the people of God with lies and accusations. When he is coming after you, fight back! Speak the Word! It is a powerful and active weapon that God has given you. Use it!

If you have lost your job, do not panic and do not let fear paralyze you! Say what the Word says about your situation. When faced

31

with adversity or impossible situations, declare, *"But my God shall supply all your need according to his riches in glory by Christ Jesus."* (Ephesians 4:19).

If you are sick, do not lose hope and allow the sickness or disease defeat you! Speak the Word, "Who his own self bare our sins in his own body on the tree, that we, being dead to sins, should live unto righteousness: by whose stripes ye were healed." (1 Peter 2:24). If you are confused, remember what the Word of God says, *"For God is not the author of confusion, but of peace..."* (1 Corinthians 14:33).

If you are feeling condemned, confess the truth of God's Word. "There is therefore now no condemnation to them which are in Christ Jesus, who walk not after the flesh, but after the Spirit." (Romans 8:1).

As you read the Scriptures, take time to speak it aloud. By doing so, you will reinforce what your eyes see and your mind processes. When you get up in the morning, speak the Word of God into your spirit. Write down the promises you need for that day and speak them into your spirit. Your heart will be encouraged, and your faith will be strengthened. You *choose* to believe what you say. If you say the same thing the devil says, you are choosing to believe a lie and speaking curses on yourself and others.

However, if you speak the Word, you are choosing to believe the truth and speak blessings. You cannot do both and please the Lord. James 3:10 says, *"Out of the same mouth proceedeth blessing and cursing. My brethren, these things ought not to be so."* Your words are powerful, and God will hold you accountable for them.

Some parents tell their children, "Do not touch matches because you will burn yourself. Do not step out into the street because a huge truck could run you over and kill you. Don't touch electricity because it will electrocute you." They take everything they do not want their children to do and turn it into a curse, "If you disobey me, something bad will happen to you." What they are really doing is giving their children a spirit of fear.

Of course, you need to teach your children the difference between what is harmless and what is dangerous. God can give you the wisdom to do that in a way that blesses—and protects—your children.

Avoid making negative confessions and speak positively! Speak the Word of God over yourself, over your children, and over other people. You will turn curses into blessings if you do!

Winning with Words

When God created the universe, He did not look down and say, "I hope there will be light," or "If there was light, it would be nice." God spoke, and there was light. God creates with His Word. In the spirit realm, your words are powerful weapons that can drive evil spirits away. They can bring deliverance and healing. Your words are agents of discernment and revelation, and expressions of faith. Do not waste your words by agreeing with Satan! God wants you to use *your* words to fight battles!

When I first learned this truth, I implemented this practice every day. I did not have a ministry to work with or great financial resources. No one knew me or believed in me. But, I had the Word of God, and I confessed it faithfully. I *received* and *proclaimed* God's Word over every area of my life. I said, "Thank You, Father, for blessing me. You are meeting all my needs. You are directing my steps. You are increasing my faith. You are helping me to understand the Word and walk in it."

My life was not controlled by my senses or by my circumstances. I did not make decisions based on my bank account, by what other people said to me, or by my emotions. Instead, I let the Word of God speak to me, and I obeyed *Him.*

There were many times when I needed a *revelation* of God's will. I needed to know His truth, not just the physical facts that affected my five senses. By believing and confessing the Word, I got the revelation I needed—and my faith was strengthened in the process.

Jesus gave us a perfect example in Mark. He saw a fig tree and cursed it. *"No man eat fruit of thee hereafter forever. And his disciples heard it"* (11:14). The next day, the disciples passed the tree and saw it was dead. *"And Peter calling to remembrance saith unto him, Master, behold, the fig tree which thou cursed is withered away; And Jesus answering saith unto them, Have faith in God."*

In the original language, that phrase means: *"Have the God kind of faith—or, mountain-moving faith"* (11:21,22).

Jesus explained, "For verily I say unto you, that whosoever shall say unto this mountain, Be thou removed, arid be thou cast into the sea; and shall not doubt in his heart, but shall believe those things which he saith shall come to pass; he shall have whatsoever he saith. Therefore, I say unto you, what things soever ye desire when ye pray, believe that ye receive them and you shall have them" (11:23-24).

Walk by Faith

Jesus said, "With this kind of faith, you can accomplish everything God tells you to do, even those things which seem impossible." Carnal Christians trust their senses to tell them what is real and what is not, but those who are spiritually mature know that relying on the five senses is limiting! From God's point of view, seeing is not believing; it's just the opposite: believing is seeing! Second Corinthians 5:7 says, *"For we walk by faith, not by sight."*

For your faith to grow, you must be in the Word. You must receive it as truth and apply it to your life. You must confess it over every area of your life, over every problem, every goal, every vision that God has given you. As your faith grows, so does your obedience. Indeed, your words and actions *feed* your faith! The more you *speak* the Word of God, the more you *hear* the revealed word of God.

If you lack vision for your life, ask God to speak to you; then begin to thank Him for directing your steps. Confess the Word over your circumstances, and stand on His promises!

If you are battling fear and unbelief, speak the Word! If you are struggling financially, speak the Word! If you are fighting for your family, speak the Word! If you are trying to resist sickness and disease, speak the Word! Wherever you are insufficient, you will find the provision you need in the Word. Speak it boldly, and believe it is already settled in the spiritual realm—whether or not you see it in the natural.

The Word of God says, "By His stripes, you were healed." Why does it say that? Is God denying the reality of sickness and disease? No, of course not. It simply means God's Word is more powerful than any sickness or disease.

If you are sick right now, pray this prayer:

"Dear God, You said I was healed by Jesus' wounds and His death on the cross. You said the same power that raised Jesus from the dead is in me. Now I declare in Jesus' name that I am healed. Your Word says I am healed, and You don't lie. Thank You for loving me and making me well."

No matter what you feel or see, *stand* on the promise of God's Word. You may or may not experience an immediate healing. That is all right. God is still in control. Stay under the care of your physician, but expect God to work a miracle in your body. Thank Him every day—and continue to confess the Word!

Six Thousand Promises

God loves you, and He wants to bless you. He doesn't want you to live in fear and bondage. He wants you to walk in freedom and uncompromising faith. He has given you everything you need to succeed: new life in Jesus, power in the Holy Spirit, the acceptance of the Father—and His unchanging, authoritative Word.

Do you realize you have 6,000 promises at your disposal? You do!

Six thousand! That's a lot of promises! When you start believing those promises and declaring them as truth for every part of your life, you will experience mountain-moving faith.

Mark 5 tells the story of a woman who had been sick for seven years with an issue of blood. Although she was considered unclean by the religious people of her day, she still came to Jesus. She was desperate for help. She had spent everything she had trying to get well, but nothing had worked; in fact, she had grown worse.

Verses 27and 28 say she pressed in through the crowd to reach Jesus, for she said, *"If I may but touch his clothes, I shall be whole."*

She did not say, "I might be healed", or "I might get better." She said, "I shall be whole." Verse 29 says, *"And straightway the fountain of her blood was dried up; and she felt in her body that she was healed of that plague."*

She dared to believe Jesus loved her enough to heal her, so she reached out and touched the hem of His garment. Her faith moved her to action, and she was healed.

One of the biggest problems you will face as you step out in faith is the temptation to listen to skeptics. The woman in Mark 5 could have listened to the crowd. She could have let critics and unbelievers intimidate her, but she did not. Instead, she focused her attention on Jesus and His ability and desire to heal her.

"In the world you have tribulations and trials and distress and frustration; but be of good cheer—take courage, be confident, certain, undaunted—for I have overcome the world. I have deprived it of power to harm, have conquered it for you" (John 16:33, Amplified).

If Jesus has conquered the world for you, then you don't have to be afraid to walk in faith!

Fear Versus Faith

I once heard the late Dr. Ed Cole, founder of Christian Men's Network, say that fear and faith share the same definition. They both mean that you believe what you have not seen will come to pass. The difference is that fear comes from the devil, and faith comes from the Lord. James 4:7, *"Stand firm against the devil; resist him and he will flee from you"* (Amplified). Satan uses fear to paralyze Christians, causing many to think they have been disqualified for service in the kingdom of God. That is why faith is so important. Fear and faith *cannot* exist together. In order for the devil to defeat you, he has to make you fearful. He will never defeat you if you are walking in faith.

But, you cannot base faith on what your senses tell you. You have to believe God, no matter what you see or hear. You have to stand on His promises, regardless of your circumstances. You have to declare His truth, even when everyone else is speaking lies. Faith will expose fear for what it is: a roaring, *toothless* lion—but *you* have to believe and speak the Word!

Hebrews 11 is a sort of "Spiritual Who's Who," and it lists Abraham as one of the great heroes of faith.

"By faith Abraham, when he was called to go out into a place which he should after receive for an inheritance, obeyed; and he went out, not knowing whither he went. By faith, he sojourned in the land of promise, as in a strange country, dwelling in tabernacles with Isaac and Jacob, the heirs with him of the same promise; For he looked for a city which hath foundations, whose builder and maker is God" (11:8-10).

"By faith Abraham, when he was tried, offered up Isaac; and he that had received the promises offered up his only begotten son, Of whom it was said, That in Isaac shall thy seed by called: Accounting that God was able to raise him up, even from the dead; from whence also he received him in a figure" (11:17-19).

"He staggered not at the promise of God through unbelief; but was strong in faith, giving glory to God; and being fully persuaded that, what he had promised, he was able also to perform. And therefore it was imputed to him for righteousness" (11:20-22).

Abraham was a man of tremendous faith. Abraham believed God more than he believed his senses, his circumstances, or his peers. He believed he would have a son, even though he and Sarah were very old. He believed he would be the father of many nations, just as God had promised.

Then, when God asked Abraham to sacrifice Isaac, the son of promise, Abraham demonstrated his faith even further. He believed God would keep His word and bless the world through Isaac, even if it meant raising him from the dead.

Abraham's faith meant more to God than anything else he could have said or done. It was so important, in fact, that the Bible says it *justified* him before the Lord. Romans 4:3 says, *"For what saith the scripture? Abraham believed God, and it was counted unto him for righteousness."*

Abraham was asked to believe unseen truths and do the impossible. He could have said no. He could have given in to fear. He could have listened to the skeptics. But he didn't—and you are blessed today because he dared to believe God and stand on the Word.

Proverbs 1:33 says, *"But whoso hearkeneth unto me shall dwell safely, and shall be quiet from fear of evil."* One of the words used for *"fear" in Hebrew means "an attendant or life companion."*

If you do not operate in faith, your life companion will be fear. Choose faith! Choose freedom in Jesus! You don't have to be victimized by fear any longer! Don't let Satan disarm you! Stand up and resist the enemy! Speak the Word, and watch him flee!

The Children's Bread

The Bible tells a dramatic story of faith and courage when a Gentile woman fell at the feet of Jesus and begged Him to cast a demon out of her daughter. *"For a certain woman, whose young daughter had an unclean spirit, heard of him, and came and fell at his feet: The woman was a Greek, a Syrophoenician by nation; and she besought him that he would cast forth the devil out of her daughter. But Jesus said unto her, Let the children first be filled: for it is not meet to take the children's bread, and to cast it unto the dogs. And she answered and said unto him, Yes, Lord: yet the dogs under the table eat of the children's crumbs. And he said unto her, For this saying go thy way; the devil is gone out of thy daughter"* (Mark 7:25-29).

Her faith was tested when Jesus told her He had been sent to the Jews first, the "children" of Israel. But she didn't give up. Instead, she replied, *"Even the dogs under the table get to eat the crumbs."* In other words, "Jesus, Your leftovers are good enough for me!" Her faith touched the heart of Jesus and moved Him to act on her behalf. With only a word, He set her daughter free.

As a Christian, you are a child of God. You have a right to the Bread of Life! You don't have to settle for crumbs—but like the Syrophoenician woman, you must ask in faith and expect to receive. Do not allow your circumstances, emotions or senses to dictate your future. God's Word is *forever* settled in heaven. As a Believer, you cannot put your faith in your senses, bank account, family, or friends. Do not trust your experience or intellect. Trust God and His Word! And by faith, speak to that mountain and say, "Move, in Jesus' name!"

Go ahead! Step out in faith. Dare to believe the Word. Your faith is important to God. He *loves* you! He *wants* to deliver you from fear and lead you into a life of uncompromising faith! The choice is yours!

CHAPTER FIVE

Fight the Good Fight of Faith

*You will have battles to fight. You are called to be a
faithful solder in the army of God. But remember,
God is in control.*

Being a Christian does not mean you are problem-free. Even though you are a child of God, it does not mean you will not come under spiritual attack. You will still have to deal with difficult situations throughout your life. No matter what you do, you will have to stand against the attacks of the devil.

God has promised the Believer that battles and persecution will come. He will have to fight deception and be on guard against unforgiveness and bitterness. He will have to fight unbelief and dislodge fear before it disarms him, making him vulnerable to further assaults.

When deception, unforgiveness, bitterness, or unbelief knocks at your heart's door, you must allow faith to answer it. When fear knocks, faith must respond.

Warfare Can Make You Better

When a Kingdom man is engaged in a battle, it does not make him bitter; it makes him better. The battle may be long and hard, but he is a *persistent* man of faith. He sees beyond the immediate skirmish to greater victory ahead.

He *learns* from his days in the trenches. The conflicts allow the Lord to hone the rough edges in his life and learn what it means to walk in submission to the King, and authority over the enemy. Spiritual warfare makes a Christian more sensitive to the Holy Spirit! By relying on Him when times are tough, he learns to love others more.

You need to see people through His eyes, and respond with a heart of faith and generosity. You also begin to listen to His voice in a more concentrated manner, and when He speaks, obey. Sometimes the Holy Spirit speaks specifically through His Word and other times through other people, or circumstances. Sometimes, He speaks through dreams and visions. Your dependence on His voice is what will get you through the heat of battle. Battles teach you to listen as you never have, and enable you to overcome.

Faith Says, "We Can Do It!"

Remember Joshua and Caleb? God promised to bring the children of Israel into a fertile land of blessing, a land filled with milk and honey. He encouraged them to be bold and to take it in His name.

Numbers 13:1 says that when the people arrived at the border, God told them to send spies into the land to examine it. Sometimes, God will give you a foretaste of the blessings He intends you to have. At the same time, when you get a glimpse of the battles that lie ahead, He will test your faith.

Moses tells the ten spies, *"...see the land, what it is; and the people that dwelleth therein, whether they be strong or weak, few or many; and what the land is that they dwell in, whether it be good or bad; and what cities they be that they dwell in, whether in tents, or in strong holds; and what the land is, whether it be fat or lean, whether there be wood therein, or not. And be ye of good courage, and bring of the fruit of the land. Now the time was the time of the firstripe grapes"* (Numbers 13:18-21).

After 40 days, the spies returned from their mission, carrying a cluster of grapes so big *"they bare it between two upon a staff."* They also brought back pomegranates and figs. It was indeed a land of great wealth and promise!

Yet despite the bounty, they saw in the land, eight of the ten men quaked with fear! God had not said anything about fighting giants! "And they told him, and said, We came unto the land whither thou sentest us, and surely it floweth with milk and honey; and this is the fruit of it. Nevertheless the people be strong that dwell in the land, and the cities are walled, and very great: and moreover we saw the children of Anak there" (Numbers 13:27-28).

Fear gripped their hearts. Isn't that the way fear works? Fear is incredibly infectious, just like a terrible sickness. That is why faith is so important. Verse 30 says, *"And Caleb stilled the people before Moses, and said, Let us go up at once, and possess it; for we are well able to overcome it."*

Joshua and Caleb stood up to the fearful spies and rebuked them for their unbelief. They were supposed to be people of faith. These two generals did not forget their days in slavery and were thankful to be delivered by a great and loving God. They had been protected from the plagues and disasters God sent to Egypt to force Pharaoh to let them go. They had seen God part the Red Sea and save them from the wrath of the Egyptians. Then, they watched God drown Pharaoh and the entire Egyptian army in the sea. Repeatedly, they had seen the mighty hand of God move on their behalf.

Joshua and Caleb knew they could take the land because of God's faithfulness. He had promised to fight their battles—even battles against giants. Numbers 14:7-9 says, *"And they spake unto all the company of the children of Israel, saying, The land, which we passed through to search it, is an exceeding good land. If the Lord delight in us, then he will bring us into this land, and give it us; a land which floweth with milk and honey. Only rebel not ye against the Lord, neither fear ye the people of the land; for they are bread for us: their defense is departed from them, and the Lord is with us: fear them not."*

Still, the people chose to believe a wicked report from the fearful majority rather than trust God's promise of success from a faith-filled minority. The people actually threatened to stone Joshua and Caleb—and begged Moses to allow them to return to Egyptian slavery! For their rebellion, God made the children of Israel wander in the wilderness 40 years, until all the fearful, unbelieving people had died. Of that generation, men and women aged 20 and older, only Joshua and Caleb remained.

The Lord spared them because they demonstrated unyielding faith and obedience, and they were blessed for it. However, they also had to wander with the unbelieving masses in the desert. For 40 years, they put their dreams on hold. For 40 years, they waited for the promise to be fulfilled. And for 40 years, they continued to trust the Lord.

Unlike the rebellious children of Israel, Joshua and Caleb were *strengthened* in the wilderness. Their character was developed, faith strengthened, and their obedience sharpened. When they walked from the wilderness across to Jordan into the land of Canaan, Joshua and Caleb were *mighty* men of God.

Joshua was singled out to lead the people of Israel into the Promised Land after Moses died. Deuteronomy 34:9 says, *"And Joshua the son of Nun was full of the spirit of wisdom; for Moses had laid his hands upon him: and the children of Israel hearkened unto him, and did as the Lord commanded Moses."*

Caleb was likewise blessed. Forty-five years after he and Joshua had spied out the land, Caleb was on the verge of inheriting God's promise to him. *"As yet I am as strong this day as I was in the day that Moses sent me: as my strength was then, even so is my strength now, for war, both to go out, and to come in. Now therefore give me this mountain, whereof the Lord spake in that day; for thou heardest in that day how the Anakims were there, and that the cities were great and fenced: if so be the Lord will be with me, then I shall be able to drive them out, as the Lord said. And Joshua blessed him, and gave unto Caleb the son of Jephunneh Hebron for an inheritance"* (Joshua 14:11-13).

Isn't it interesting that Caleb wanted to capture the same land he had seen in his younger days? The giants were still there, but they did not frighten him. He knew more than ever that God is a good God who is able and willing to deliver His people from the hand of the enemy.

Strengthen Yourself

As a new generation of Israelites gathered on the banks of the Jordan to march into the Promised Land, Joshua cautioned the people to get ready for the battles ahead. Joshua 1:11 says, *"Pass through the host, and command the people, saying, Prepare you victuals; for within three days ye shall pass over this Jordan, to go in to possess the land, which the Lord your God giveth you to possess it."*

The word "victuals" means "meat, food, or provision." In other words, strengthen yourself. As a Christian, you are called to fight the good fight of faith. But you cannot meet the enemy unprepared! You must strengthen yourself, but not with physical food. Deuteronomy 8:3 says, *"...man doth not live by bread only, but by every word that proceedeth out of the mouth of the Lord doth man live."*

Then, put on the armor and prepare to meet the unseen enemy! Ephesians 6:10-17 says, *"Finally, my brethren, be strong in the Lord, and in the power of his might. Put on the whole armour of God, that ye may be able to stand against the wiles of the devil. For we wrestle not against flesh and blood, but against principalities, against powers, against the rulers of the darkness of this world, against spiritual wickedness in high places. Wherefore take unto you the whole armour of God, that ye may be able to withstand in the evil day, and having done all, to stand. Stand therefore, having your loins girt about with truth, and having on the breastplate of righteousness; And your feet shod with the preparation of the gospel of peace; Above all, taking the shield of faith, wherewith ye shall be able to quench all the fiery darts of the wicked. And take the helmet of salvation, and the sword of the Spirit, which is the word of God."*

Eyes of Faith

I will never forget the time God told me to go to Israel one Easter. I did not really know why, but He assured me it would be worth my time and effort. When I arrived, I was both excited and full of faith.

I got up early that Easter morning to pray, and God spoke to my heart, "You are going to see a mighty breakthrough in this nation, and it is going to happen today."

Then, the Holy Spirit told me to go to the Lord's tomb. When I got there, long lines stretched from the buses all the way to the site. Everybody wanted to be there for the Easter morning communion.

The Holy Spirit told me to stay at the tomb. Then He said, "The man in front of you is going to be used as an instrument to bring a mighty miracle to pass. This is in relation to what I have called you here to do."

I still did not know what God had planned, but I said, "Good Morning" to the man ahead of me all the same.

He turned around, and I noticed that he was wearing old, baggy pants and had dirty glasses. He looked at me and said in a low voice,

"How are you doing, Reverend Evans?"

"Real fine," I replied. Then, I looked closer. I could not believe my eyes. "Bunker Hunt?" I asked. "What are you doing in Israel?"

He said, "It's the first time I have ever been here. I just sort of sneaked in."

"You know I deal in oil with the Arab countries," he continued, "and it is not good for my business to come to Israel. But I wanted to see Jesus' tomb, because I recently invited Him into my heart."

Then he asked why I was in Israel, but I could not tell him. It felt strange to have one of the wealthiest men in the world ask about my mission and have to answer, "I don't know."

I told him if he really wanted to know, to call me at my hotel that night. Wasn't that a dumb thing to say? Why would anyone want to call me at night just to ask me why I was in Israel?

A Money Crisis

Later that day, I went to Haifa. I was with the senior advisor to the prime minister of Israel at conference with presidents representing every university in Israel, and with six other men on the 27th floor of Haifa University. Out our window, we could see Nazareth and Mount Megiddo, or as it is called in the Bible, Armageddon.

They said, "It all began there, and it will all end there. We have a great crisis. All our money is gone. We have no funds to run our universities. They will all be shut down by 9:00 a.m. tomorrow if something does not change."

"Have you prayed?" I asked. They said they had not, and that their negotiations over the last few months had produced few results.

We formed a circle, grasped hands, and I prayed. In faith, I asked God to provide the money and thanked Him in the name of Jesus.

Within six hours, the money was released! One of the university presidents called me later. He asked if I could recommend someone to be on the founding board of Haifa University. He was grateful for my help and wanted to repay me somehow.

Would I be interested, he wondered, in speaking at the university every year? He also said I could distribute 70,000 Bibles and other books at the university. They would sneak them in!

That night when I got back to the hotel, Bunker Hunt called me wanting to know why I was in Israel. I told him I was there because God wanted to open the doors of the universities for the gospel. I told him what happened, and he said, "That is very substantial. Could I invest in it?"

I learned the importance of seeing with eyes of faith. God may tell you to do something you do not understand, and that is when your faith *must* be strong. If you only respond to those requests that make sense in the natural, then you will miss many tremendous blessings—and you will miss being used by God to bless others for the sake of Christ.

God Opens the Doors

This is a long story, but I want to share just a part of it to show you how God can work in amazing ways when you see what He sees—like Rahab.

In Joshua 2:9 and 11, Rahab said, "... *I know that the Lord had given you the land... for the Lord your God, he is God in heaven above, and in earth beneath.*"

From a human perspective, Rahab had every reason to believe that Jericho was safe. It was a well-fortified city, and she lived in a house on the wall. Indeed, she lived in a fortress. The king's military was strong, and it was ready to fight from the inside out.

Still, something stirred her and she opened her doors to enemy spies. She really did not have any reason to believe God would protect her. She did not know the God of Israel. She had not been taught to see the impending battle from His vantage point. But there was something about the men who stayed at her house that was different. There was something *powerful* about their God.

She had heard stories about the Israelis' miraculous escape from the Egyptians. She knew God had actually parted the Red Sea so they could cross to safety. She knew they had utterly defeated two mighty Amorite kings, Sihon and Og. And she knew the spies were men of honor. When they promised to save her life and the lives of her family members, she believed them.

Rahab made a choice to believe God. She made a choice to receive His promise, and with that choice came the ability to see with eyes of faith.

If you are fighting the good fight of faith, you have to believe God and receive His promise to you. Only then will you see with eyes of faith. You cannot be a people-pleaser. You must not listen to the words of men and embrace them as supreme truth. You must see with the eyes of the Spirit, and hear with your heart.

You cannot control what people do to you, but you *can* control your response. Proverbs 16:7 says, "When a man's ways please the Lord, he maketh even his enemies to be at peace with him." Rahab responded in faith, and God used her enemies to save her—and her family.

Faith in God's Word

Rahab was obedient to God. The Bible says her heart was open to the Lord, but it also says she had more faith in God's words than in man's words.

If you intend to fight the good fight of faith, you must trust the Word of God. The words of men may stir you to action. They may encourage you. But they should never be the *final* word for your life. The Word of God is light for your path. It is health for your flesh. It is the revealed will of God for your life.

If you value the words of men over the Word of God, you violate His work in your life. You leave yourself open to temptation and deception. For a Christian, discernment is grounded in the Word of God. Without it to guide your steps, you are vulnerable to demonic attack.

Rahab heard that God's Word was eternal. It carried authority and power. It was supernatural and accessible. She heard the reports and believed the Word—and from that position of faith, she was able to act in a wise and courageous manner. Rahab's response to the challenges she faced was to obey the Word of God. You must be careful to do the same.

You are living in a world where spiritual winds are blowing all around you, and you must know which spirit is speaking. Is it the Spirit of God? Or, is a spirit of deception trying to trap you?

There is a spirit of rebellion and discontent in the world, and it is described in Second Timothy 3:1-5, *"This know also, that in the last days perilous times shall come. For men shall be lovers of their own selves, covetous, boasters, proud, blasphemers, disobedient to parents, unthankful, unholy, Without natural affection, trucebreakers, false accusers, incontinent, fierce, despisers of those that are good, Traitors, heady, high-minded, lovers of pleasures more than lovers of God; Having a form of godliness, but denying the power thereof: from such turn away."*

You must be alert! Be wise! God's Word is a powerful—and living—tool that can help bring you to maturity.

Ephesians 4:13-14 says, *"Till we all come in the unity of the faith, and of the knowledge of the Son of God, unto a perfect man, unto the measure of the stature of the fullness of Christ: That we henceforth be no more children, tossed to and fro, and carried about with every wind of doctrine, by the sleight of men, and cunning craftiness, whereby they lie in wait to deceive."*

The next time someone tries to persuade you to go against the Word of God, ask yourself, "If I listen to this and receive it as truth, will it make me a better person? Will it make me more like Jesus?" Rahab chose to stand on the Word of God, no matter what anyone else said. She acted in faith, and was saved as a result.

Characteristics to Avoid

Rahab was a woman whose faith you should emulate, but there are numerous Bible characters whose mistakes you should avoid:

1. *The Jonah Jog.* Jonah's was a sorry, half-hearted commitment. God told him to go to Nineveh and preach repentance, but he did not quite make it. He said, "I started to go. At least, I made the attempt."

   Many Christians today are like Jonah—they are committed in word but not in deed. What about you? When God tells you to do something, do you run away? Or, do you answer a resilient "Yes!" and move ahead with a heart full of faith?

2. *The Samson Smile.* Samson was a man of great strength but limited wisdom. He trusted his own strength, instead of God's Word. As a result, he became prideful and smug. He taunted the enemy. He tempted a woman whose sole purpose was to destroy him. He let his emotions get in the way of God's purpose for his life, and he paid dearly for it.

   Where is your heart today? Are you letting your emotions betray you? Or, are you standing on the truth of the Word. Samson was self-confident; what about you? Are you putting your confidence in self, or are you trusting in God?

3. *The Absalom Ambition.* Absalom wanted to lead the people of Israel. He wanted to be in control. He was not content to follow his father, so he compromised with the enemy. He brought rebellion and confusion to the land, and he tore the kingdom in half.

   Are you letting ambition drive you to rebellion? Are you complaining and plotting against the authority God has put over you in your church, your home, your work? Or, are you willing to submit and pray for those in authority over you? Are you willing to wait for God to release the anointing in your life at the right time and in the right way?

4. *The Moab Motto.* Moab was a nasty human being who was born out of an incestuous relationship between Lot and his daughter. His was an attitude found in Sodom and Gomorrah, "Go ahead, push beyond the limits God has set. Whatever you do is all right. Whatever you say is okay. No one is going to hold you accountable."

Is this your way of thinking: "I don't have to stay within the boundaries God set. Those boundaries are for other people. I can commit this particular sin and get away with it. I'm too smart to get caught."

God set limits for you because He loves you. Those boundaries are for your protection and joy. God cares about you! He cares so much He allowed His only Son to die for your sin! God cares, and He *will* hold you accountable for your actions!

5. *The Achan Acorn.* I was out raking leaves many years ago, and when I finished, I looked around at the yard and thought how pretty it was. The grass was so perfect.

I put my rake down and felt so good about what I had done. As I started across the grass, I slipped on an acorn and almost broke my back.

One little acorn! Achan had that same attitude about sin. He said[1], "It is just one sin. No one will notice."

Do you try to hide things from God? Do you say: "It's just a little infraction. I can keep it a secret. I'm not really hurting anyone." Or, do you allow God to search your heart, to cleanse it, and fill it with His Spirit?

6. *The Herod Halo.* Herod loved the praises of men. He was ob-

sessed with the idea of earthly success. He was so consumed with himself that he was willing to sacrifice the Son of God to gain favor with the majority.

Are you sacrificing your faith to win the praises of men? Or, are you willing to stand on your own and be counted as a warrior of faith?

7. *The Pilot Perfume.* "My hands are clean," Pilot said. "I haven't done anything wrong. Blame it on the Pharisees, if you want, but don't point your finger at me!"

Are you denying any sin in your life? Are you playing the "Blame Game"? Or, are you confessing your sin and allowing Him to renew your mind and wash you "white as snow"?

God Controls the Battle

Remember this; you will have battles to fight. You are called to be a faithful soldier in the army of God. But remember, God is in control.

God will allow you to face the enemy in order to help you grow. He wants you to mature as a Christian! He wants your faith to be strong! He wants you to be wise!

He will never ask you to fight in your own strength or wisdom. He is fighting the good fight *with* you! He is fighting the good fight *for* you! Jesus fought the war against sin, sickness, death, and hell—and He won! Colossians 2:15 says, *"And having spoiled principalities and powers, he made a show of them openly, triumphing over them in it."*

Be encouraged! Be strong in the Lord and in the power of His might. Put on the whole armor of God. Then, stand firm on His Word, and know that your battle is His.

CHAPTER SIX

Stop Worrying—Forever

What is worry? Misplaced faith, faith in fear, or a lack of faith in God's ability.

I read somewhere that more than half of all the diseases in the world are caused by worry. Think of it. More than half of all the diseases in the world! Have you ever seen a person whose hands, for instance, were twisted because of rheumatoid arthritis? Research seems to indicate that arthritis is caused, at least partially, by fear and anxiety. These are emotions that cause the body to release poisons into the system.

Far too many Christians today are filled with worry. They worry about money. They worry about job security. They worry about their safety. They worry about their health. They worry about their future. Matthew 6:33 says, *"But seek ye first the kingdom of God, and his righteousness; and all these things shall be added unto you."*

God never intended you to live a life of worry and stress! He wants you to walk in faith and liberty! He has made you an overcomer. So, why don't you feel like one? Why do the cares of this world weigh heavily upon your shoulders? Because you are carrying them on *your* shoulders. The secret of a worry-free life is seeking God's kingdom and His righteousness first, before everything else.

Abraham Sought His Kingdom

Abraham was a man who refused to worry. Hebrews 11:8 says, *"By faith Abraham, when he was called to go out into a place which he should after receive for an inheritance, obeyed; and he went out, not knowing whither he went."* He had no idea where he was going, but he refused to worry! God had promised to bless him and his family, and that was enough.

In Genesis 12:2-3, God said, *"And I will make of thee a great nation, and I will bless thee, and make thy name great; and thou shalt be a blessing: And I will bless them that bless thee, and curse him that curseth thee: and in thee shall all families of the earth be blessed."*

Look again at this promise for a moment:

1. God said He would make of Abraham a great nation.
2. He said He would make Abraham's name great.
3. He said Abraham would be a blessing.
4. He promised to bless those who blessed Him, and curse those who cursed Him.
5. He said all families of the earth would be blessed because of Abraham's faithfulness.

What a promise!

Notice that God never said, "Abraham, *you* will create a mighty nation. *You* will make your name great. *You* will make yourself a blessing." No, the responsibility to birth a nation, to honor a man, to anoint him, to bless his friends and curse his enemies, and to bless the world's families rested with God, not Abraham. That is because the Lord made a covenant, or contract, with Abraham.

God was not looking for a helper when He called Abraham; He was looking for a friend. He wanted to share His heart with him. He wanted to instill within him an appreciation for the things of the Spirit. He wanted to give him vision and a sense of destiny.

That is precisely what God wants to do for *you*. He wants you to be His friend. He wants to open your heart to spiritual truths. He wants to give you renewed vision. He wants to reveal His destiny for your life.

God wanted Abraham to seek His kingdom *first,* and according to Scripture, he did. Hebrews 11:10 says, *"For he looked for a city which hath foundations, whose builder and maker is God."*

As he walked with God, Abraham discovered a number of things about His kingdom:

1. The kingdom of God is eternal; it will outlive all of man's kingdoms.
2. The kingdom of God operates in wisdom, grace, and truth; deception and confusion are exposed.
3. The kingdom of God is based on love, mercy, and generosity; there is no room for self-promotion.
4. The kingdom of God is a safe place; there is no need to fear rejection.
5. The kingdom of God is full of provision; every need is met.

You can apply these truths to your life. You *must* seek the kingdom of God *first.* Then, you will see your plans, visions, and dreams fall into place. Stop worrying about the future! Stop worrying about your failures! Stop worrying about *your* kingdom! The kingdom of God will survive when your kingdom crumbles.

Abraham learned another important lesson about the kingdom. He saw that being a citizen of the kingdom did not grant him immunity from trouble. Repeatedly, he had to deal with difficulties. Some were major problems, but he confronted them as a man of faith. He did not always make the right decision either. Sometimes, he made mistakes—but he never lost sight of the kingdom or the God he served.

When you experience upheavals in your life, look to the Lord and know there is peace in the midst of the storm, peace that passes human understanding.

In time, you will see your faith grow, and you will realize that not all the things you have been worrying about are so frightening after all. They may be challenges, to be sure; they may be obstacles—but God has *allowed* you to walk through this period of struggle for a reason. He wants your faith to grow. He wants to develop your patience and character. He wants you to be more like Jesus.

If you will seek His kingdom first, you will be delivered from worry!

Heirs of Righteousness

How would you like to have the kind of relationship with God that Abraham had? Well, I have news for you—you *do*. You are an heir to the blessings of Abraham! You are an heir by faith! Galatians 3:29 says, *"And if ye be Christ's, then are ye Abraham's seed, and heirs according to the promise."*

Isn't that wonderful news? You are in covenant with God because of your faith in Jesus! You are entitled to all the blessings God promised Abraham. You are a citizen of His kingdom, and an heir to the promise! But, you must seek His kingdom first—*and* His righteousness.

What is God's righteousness? To put it simply, it is Jesus Christ. He is the righteousness of God, and by faith, you are made righteous *in Him.* Jesus' death and resurrection brought life to you, both abundant and eternal. It also gave you favor with God the Father. Second Corinthians 5:21 says, *"For he hath made him to be sin for us, who knew no sin; that we might be made the righteousness of God in him."*

Isn't that amazing? You have the resurrected life of Jesus in your spirit, along with His power, authority, wisdom, and anointing. You are equipped to do His will. You are loved and called, purified and blessed— because of your relationship with Jesus!

Luke 10:38-42 tells of a time when Jesus was passing through a town, and He stopped to visit with Mary and Martha. Immediately, Martha began pulling the house together and preparing dinner. Mary, on the other hand, sat at Jesus' feet and listened to Him teach.

When Martha saw her sister just sitting there, she became angry. But Jesus rebuked her and, in verses 41and 42, He said, "...*Martha, Martha, you are worried and bothered about so many things; but only a few things are necessary, really only one, for Mary has chosen the good part, which shall not be taken away from her.*" (NASB).

The world is full of distractions. All around you are things that vie for your time and attention. You may feel pulled in a multitude of directions—but you do not have to live like that. You can draw close to Jesus. You can seek Him first. He *wants* you to stop all the busy work and sit for a while at His feet He *wants* you to listen and obey.

God wants you to receive His love. For it is out of *intimacy* you will begin to seek Him first. Your passion for Jesus will cause you to seek His face every morning, throughout the day and when you go to bed at night. Your desire to *know* Him will prompt you to put His kingdom ahead of your own, and as you do, all the other things in your life will fall into place.

Believe in the Promise

The Bible says Abraham believed God. Think about that for a moment. Abraham did not know where God was leading him. All he knew was that God had said, "Go, and I will bless you." Abraham could have let fear paralyze him. He could have worried about his future. He could have planted himself in one spot and refused to go any further until God explained what He was doing. But he didn't.

Abraham believed God. He did not allow worry or fear to distract him from his call and destiny. Romans 4:20-21 says, "*He staggered not at the promise of God through unbelief; but was strong in faith, giving glory to God; And being fully persuaded that, what he had promised, he was able also to perform."*

Who had given Abraham the promise? God. Who was going to perform it? God. Then, what was there to worry about? Absolutely nothing.

Philippians 4:6 says, *"Be careful for nothing; but in everything by prayer and supplication with thanksgiving let your requests be made known unto God."*

God does not want you to worry—not about your job, or family, or finances! He does not want you to worry about *anything*. He wants you to trust Him. When you fall into a spirit of worry, you become fearful and defensive. You lose your joy and your sense of peace. Even worse, you become unproductive in the kingdom.

But, when you seek God's kingdom first, and draw close to Jesus, you break down the walls that keep you from ministering to God and to others. You open yourself up so the Lord can use you to touch hurting people, and in the process, *you* are restored, renewed, and strengthened. John 14:27 says, *"Peace I leave with you, my peace I give unto you: not as the world giveth, give I unto you. Let not your heart be troubled, neither let it be afraid."* How can you avoid letting your heart be troubled? By seeking the kingdom of God and His righteousness. In every decision, ask yourself this question, "Am I seeking the kingdom of God first, or am I seeking to further my own kingdom?"

Seasons of Barrenness

Many people believe they have been disqualified as Christians because they are going through a period of barrenness. Perhaps you are experiencing barrenness in your life today. You have lost your joy. You cannot seem to motivate yourself to pray or read the Word. God seems remote, and you feel utterly defeated.

If this describes your life right now, be encouraged! Barrenness does not have to be permanent! God is not angry with you! He is not finished with you! Barrenness is a time of vulnerability. It is when the Enemy tries to torment, heap condemnation and confusion, and bring fear, doubt, and worry. That is when you must *stand* on the Word and *believe* that God is still at work in your life.

God is committed to finishing what He started in you! Philippians 1:6 says, *"Being confident of this very thing, that he which hath begun a good work in you will perform it until the day of Jesus Christ:"*

If you are in a season of barrenness, do not despair. God is refining your faith. He is honing your patience. He is giving you an opportunity to reach out in the emptiness and touch His heart. Romans 8:28 says, *"And we know that all things work together for good to them that love God, to them who are the called according to his purpose."*

Do you remember the story of Elizabeth? She was barren, yet she eventually gave birth to John the Baptist. In fact, a number of women in the Bible were barren for a season. Then God blessed them, opened their womb, and they became extremely fruitful. This can be your testimony, too!

When God created the earth, He told man and woman to be fruitful and multiply. The desire to be fruitful is in your heart, and when you do not *feel* fruitful, the tendency is to look within yourself for the solution. When you do not find the answer you are looking for, you begin to worry. You let your imagination run wild.

Stop! When you do not feel fruitful, ask the Lord to reveal Himself to you. Ask Him to show you His will. Then, be still and listen. Wait for God to speak.

Sometimes when God is silent, you take that to mean He has turned His back on you. You feel barren and alone. Nevertheless, think about this: you may not be *hearing* the voice of God simply because He is being quiet. God wants you to be still and *know* that He is God. When the Lord is silent, listen up! He is probably saying something very important to you.

Barrenness is not a sign that God has forsaken you. He has promised never to leave or forsake you. However, barrenness *can* be an indication that you need to seek the Lord. You need to press in to Him as a child snuggles in the arms of his daddy.

When seasons of barrenness come, panic can develop in the mind of a Believer. He feels an incredible urge to *do something*. "God doesn't seem to be moving, so I'm just going to have to jump start things a bit," he says. Where does that attitude come from? Certainly not the Lord. He never rushes into anything.

When you are feeling desperate, just realize the enemy is pushing your buttons. Think about it for a moment; the devil has convinced Americans they have to move quicker, work harder, be smarter, and do more. God, on the other hand, urges you to *wait*. "Wait," He says, "and see what miracles I will do on your behalf."

Fruit Comes by Faith

First Samuel tells the story of Hannah. It is a sad story about a wonderful woman who was in a period of barrenness. She asked God to bless her with a child. Although she did not know it at the time, God had something fantastic in store for Hannah. He not only gave her a son, He gave her an *anointed* son, a baby she named Samuel. That little boy grew up to become one of the most powerful prophets who ever lived.

God chose to bless a woman others had scorned. He chose to bring fruitfulness to a woman who had wrestled for years with the shame of barrenness. In those days, barrenness was considered a curse, but God took a curse and changed it into a blessing! Hannah could not produce fruit in her own life; she had to wait on God. If you are struggling with barrenness in your life, stop striving. You cannot force fruit to grow any more than a peach tree can *force* its peaches to grow! The fruit appears when the time is right—and it stays on the tree until it is ready to be picked.

Seeking the kingdom and His righteousness moves you into faith. You cannot walk in fear and faith at the same time. You cannot live with worry and peace at the same time. If you are giving in to fear and worry, you are not seeking the kingdom of God first. Fear says, "I want results now. If God isn't going to make something happen, then I will." Faith, on the other hand, says, "God, I want Your best for my life. I am willing to wait. I am willing to be barren for a while so you can produce great fruit in my life when I am ready."

The Seed of Abraham

As a Believer, you are the seed of Abraham, and therefore, you are blessed! If you really believe that, then stop trying to manipulate God's will. Stop looking for the right contact, the right job, the right car or house or partner or church to be happy. Wait on God, and do what He says.

God wants you to enter into covenant with Him as Abraham did, in faith. Let go of fear and worry. Seek first the kingdom of God and His righteousness. Practice putting Him first. As you do, you will find the strength and wisdom you need to confront, and overcome, worry and fear.

If you are going through a time of barrenness, be patient! Seek first the kingdom of God and His righteousness. In due season, you will bring forth fruit that honors the Lord and blesses others.

Abraham spent his entire life looking for the Promised Land. He could have said, "God, I have been serving you for six months now. Where is my kingdom? Where is all that You promised me?" Did Abraham see the promise before he died? No. Hebrews 1:13 says, *"These all died in faith, not having received the promises, but having seen them afar off, and were persuaded of them, and embraced them,* *and confessed that <u>they were strangers and pilgrims</u> on the earth."* Abraham could have complained, but he did not. He just continued to trust God and obey His Word. Abraham's descendants live today because he put the kingdom of God first in his life.

Misplaced Faith

What is worry? Misplaced faith. In other words, it is faith in fear. Worry is actually your lack of confidence in God's ability to meet your needs. When you worry, you are really saying, "I am not completely convinced that God is going to take care of me in this area."

Abraham trusted God's words. What about you? Where is your trust? Is your faith weak right now? If so, open the Word of God, and let it speak to you. Study God's promises. Let them encourage you! The Bible contains over *6,000 promises* because God knows your faith needs to be strengthened!

Deuteronomy 29:9 says, *"Keep therefore the words of this covenant, and do them, that ye may prosper in all you do." If you obey the Word, you will prosper.*

God spoke, and Abraham responded in faith. How do you build your faith?

1. Be sure you are hearing the Word of God. Do not let the words of men distract and confuse you.
2. Seek the Lord with a heart of faith. Hebrews 11:6 says, *"But without faith it is impossible to please him: for he that cometh to God must believe that he is, and that he is a rewarder of them that diligently seek* him." (Emphasis added.)
3. Speak the Word. Let your heart and mouth agree with the Word, and wait for God to move.

Faith Comes by Hearing

The only way to reverse the effects of fear and worry is to speak the Word in faith. Romans 10:17 says, *"So then faith cometh by hearing, and hearing by the word of God."*

Psychologists say that before you emote, or express any emotion, you think. No emotions come before thoughts. Psychologists try to help mentally ill patients think positive thoughts to restore their negative emotions. Yet, the Bible said this was true long before psychologists discovered that it works.

The more you meditate on the Word of God, the more you believe. The more time you spend with Him, the more encouraged you feel. As your faith grows, so does your willingness to act on the truth. Your commitment to, and faith in, the Word of God will empower you to tell fear and worry to leave in Jesus' name.

Erase the Tape

Proverbs 4:20-22 says, *"Son, attend to my words. Incline thy ear unto My sayings. Let them not depart from thy eyes, keep them in the midst of thy spirit. For they are life unto those that find them, and health to all their flesh."*

Did you know you can go through cycles of depression at certain times of the year? If you experienced a crisis on a certain date several years back, you can feel the very same emotions on the same date this year, because your brain has registered something very severe and has not "erased the tape," so to speak.

Have you ever wondered why you felt depressed when there was no reason to feel bad? It is because you did not erase the tape with the Word of God.

Identify areas where the enemy has assaulted you and declare God's promises to be true instead. Allow the Word to get into your spirit and stir up your faith. The promises of God will erase the tape!

Speak the Word! The negative things in your life can be counteracted when you speak the Word. You do not have to let your brain continue to play depressing, fear-filled messages repeatedly. Speak the Word! Put your faith to work. Otherwise, you will be a victim of roller-coaster emotions. You will be happy today, depressed tomorrow. You will love the Lord one day, and be punched-out the next. Speak the Word!

You will never succeed in overcoming your complexes, inferiorities, doubts, worries, and fears by using carnal methods.

Find some promises of God that relate to you and your life and write them down. Read them aloud when you pray. Meditate on them. Psalm 1:2 says, *"But his delight is in the law of the Lord, And in his law he meditates day and night."*

"Blessed Am I"

When you meditate on God's Word, personalize it. Do not just read: "blessed be the man," but "blessed am I." Recognize that *you* are the one who is going to prosper in Jesus. *You* are the one who is being saved, filled, healed, and delivered.

Why not pray this prayer with me, and stop worrying—forever:

"Dear Jesus, I confess that worry is a sin. When I give in to worry, I am really saying You are not able to take care of me. I am giving the devil an opportunity to attack me. I'm sorry. I humble myself before You and repent of this sin.

"I refuse to walk in fear any longer—from this day forward, I choose to walk in faith. In the name of Jesus, I change my mind, I submit my thoughts to You, and I choose to speak Your Word. Please help me to meditate on the Word and declare its truth over every area of my life. Draw me to You and to Your Word. Direct my thoughts so they honor You in the morning, at noontime, and in the evening.

"I will be like a tree of life that brings forth fruit in its season.

I will not be barren forever. I will prosper, because I attend unto the words of God."

CHAPTER SEVEN

Do Not Be Bothered, Be Blessed!

*Do not listen to the lies of the devil when God
almighty paid such a great price for you to be
redeemed and to walk with dignity.*

Millions of Christians struggle with sleeping, troubled by all kinds of worries and negative thoughts. A life filled with misfortune and mistakes causes them to feel defeated, demoralized, paralyzed, and fearful. Everywhere you look, people seem to feed on bad news. They *thrive* on tragedies. So often, people try to fake or pretend to be happy, but they are in constant turmoil, fighting inward battles with no relief and no real victory.

These people are living *under* their circumstances. Problems with finances, trouble with a spouse or a child, worries about the job, and concerns for the future overshadow everything else in life, even the blessings of God. While most Christians want to live above their struggles, many are simply unable to find the root of the problems that plague them.

What is bothering you today? Identify your joy-stealer—worry, fear, or stress. Bind these spirits and speak to them. Jesus said He came that you might have life. Do not meditate on the lies of the enemy!

Be Strong

On one occasion, I received a phone call from John Osteen, Joel Osteen's father, who was a dear pastor friend of mine, and he said, "A lady who was dying of cancer came to your crusade meeting many years ago in Houston. You told the people there was a woman in the audience who was being healed right then of cancer—and she was healed. Now she's being attacked by the devil with a different disease. Will you call her and pray for her?"

I told him I would be glad to. So I did, and she was thrilled. She said, "Brother Mike, I was a dead woman over ten years ago when you prayed the prayer of faith and God totally healed me. Now the devil has come back with a different disease."

"Will you believe the Word of God?" I asked.

"Yes," She answered.

"Then let the weak say, 'I am strong,'" I replied.

She wanted to tell me all about her disease—how it was affecting her and how afraid she was. But I stopped her and instructed her to speak the Word.

I told her to repeat after me, "Let the weak say, I am strong. I am strong, I am strong, I am strong."

As she said that, the power of God fell on her. She began screaming, "I am strong, I am healed."

What happened? She got into God's glory. God said He would supply all of our needs according to His riches in glory.

Expose the Root

Do you know what is bothering you? Identify the root and move into an atmosphere where God can supply your needs. Then you can go forward into the destiny God has planned for you. But, how do you identify what is bothering you? It begins when you make a God-connection. The Apostle Paul said a band of constraining love binds God's people together. When you realize this bond with God and with fellow Christians, peace and harmony will fill your life.

Jesus began a good work on Calvary, and He will complete what He has started, Philippians 1:6 tells us, *"Being confident of this very thing, that he which hath begun a good work in you will perform it until the day of Jesus Christ."*

Identify your joy-stealers. These can be worry, fear, stress, rejection, anger, or confusion. Choose life. Do not lie in bed meditating on the lies of the Enemy. When the devil assaults your mind, resist him! Talk back to him. Identify the spirits of worry and rejection, and do not entertain them.

You must understand that you are in a war. This is not a game. The devil is accusing you before God. If he shows up at your door to accuse you, and you entertain him, it is an insult to the integrity of the cross. Do not listen to the lies of the devil when God Almighty paid such a great price for you to be redeemed and to walk with dignity.

Nothing can rob you of your hold on grace, your claim to peace or your confidence in God without your permission. The grace of God is too great. The love and mercy of God are too strong. The compassion and peace of God are too powerful; they cannot, and will not, leave you—unless you give the devil a legal right to steal it. You must believe God's Word.

Never release your grip on the covenant Christ made for you. The Bible says you walk by faith and not by sight.

The Key to Africa

Many years ago, God told me He was going to open up the world to the gospel and that we would see breakthroughs in different nations. God showed me He was opening up Africa, Asia, and the Soviet Union. At that time, He told me to go to Mexico to a specific hotel and pray.

One morning, the Lord told me to get up and stand on the sidewalk in a certain spot. He said someone would come up to me who would have the key to Africa. Little did I know, it would be Maureen Reagan and her husband, the daughter of President Ronald Reagan. They were in Mexico to rest for a couple of days before going on to the White House. They had just come back from Africa on a fact-finding mission and had met with every president on the continent. I knew none of this at the time, but the Holy Spirit did.

As they walked down the sidewalk, God said, "They are the ones. Tell them you need to talk to them about Africa." I had never even met them! I walked up, asked how they were and told them I needed to talk to them about Africa.

We sat down over a meal and I described to them a person I had seen in the Spirit. They identified him as the President of Uganda. I told them to tell him to bring his cabinet to Washington D. C. Within six weeks, the Ugandan president's cabinet was sitting in my suite, along with my wife and several other evangelical leaders.

God not only worked that situation out, but He opened up the Republic of Uganda to me. We had the greatest crusade in the history of Uganda!

Protect Your Joy

When the devil shows up at your house, you can be sure he isn't coming because he likes you. He has come to kill, steal, and destroy. You may think it is natural to be depressed at times, but Jesus was not defeated. No one in the Word was permanently defeated. They suffered every kind of difficult circumstance, but they remained more than conquerors in Christ Jesus. The devil is under your feet. Do you understand what I am saying? Choose life! Don't let the devil steal your joy.

Let me tell you something about this concept of destiny. You have to hear God to know your destiny. Destiny and hearing God have taken me all over the world. We have seen multiplied millions of people genuinely born again.

If you want to understand how to overcome what is bothering you, start guarding your words. The words that come out of your mouth create heavenly deposits in God's kingdom account. When the devil assaults your mind and gives you negative thoughts, speak the Word aloud. Line up with the Word of God, for that Word supplies your needs according to His riches in glory. You can activate it to release deposits on your interest-bearing account by your obedience through Christ.

Acknowledge Jesus as Lord

How can you overcome what is bothering you? Acknowledge Jesus as Lord. Realize that God is on the throne. Paul talks about how his circumstances turned out for the greater progress of the gospel, *"But I would ye should understand, brethren, that the things which happened unto me have fallen out rather unto the furtherance of the gospel; so that my bonds in Christ are manifest in all the palace, and in all other places; and many of the brethren in the Lord, waxing confident by my bonds, are much more bold to speak the word without fear."* (Philippians 1:12-14).

People looked at Paul and probably said something like this, "Oh you poor thing. You are in prison. You have been stoned. You have gone through all kinds of hell." Nevertheless, Paul told them not to feel sorry for him. He declared, "I am rejoicing. My circumstances have turned out for the greater progress of the gospel."

The word *"progress"* in the Greek describes pioneer woodcutters who would precede an advancing army, clearing the way of trees and brush. When the armies went through, they wanted to win a big battle. But, before they could do that, the pioneer woodcutters had to clear the way, or make "progress."

What did Paul say about his circumstances? He said they have turned out for the greater "progress" of the gospel. No matter how the devil assaulted him—because his faith was rooted in the Word of God and grounded in the Holy Ghost—he was a Holy Ghost woodcutter.

Empty Yourself

Next, to get over what is bothering you, you must empty yourself. The Bible says you are to be light in a corrupt and perverse world. Isaiah 60:1-2 says, *"Arise, shine; for thy light is come, and the glory of the Lord is risen upon thee. For, behold, the darkness shall cover the earth, and gross darkness the people: but the Lord shall arise upon thee, and his glory shall be seen upon thee."*

The *"light"* in this passage describes *us* and is a Greek word, which means *"luminaries,"* or stars. In other words, you are not merely a little light, but a star. Let me tell you about stars. I was in the former Soviet Union to conduct the first pastors' school of evangelism. I saw Russian commanders there who had binoculars, which they call starbursts.

These binoculars can pull the light off the stars and the moon. They work even better than infrared lenses. You can have a totally dark night, where neither stars nor moon can be seen, yet when you look through these binoculars, it looks like you are seeing everything in daylight. There is light you cannot see with the natural eye. An unbeliever looks around and sees that everything is bad. He sees total darkness. But, to the Believer whose faith is grounded in Jesus Christ, it looks like daytime!

Emptying yourself means taking the form of a servant and being humble, contrary to everything the world may tell you:

The wisdom of the Greeks tells you to—know yourself.

The wisdom of the Romans says—discipline yourself.

Religion tells you to—conform yourself.

Epicureanism says to—satisfy yourself.

Education tells you to—expand yourself.

Psychology says—assert yourself.

Materialism suggests that you—please yourself.

Humanism encourages you to—believe in yourself.

Pride says—promote yourself.

But Jesus Christ tells us to—humble yourself.

Forget the Past

To get over what is bothering you, stop living in the past. Close the door on what has gone before. As Paul said, forget the things that are behind you and focus on your high calling in Jesus today.

To put the past truly behind you, you must forgive anyone who has offended you. Then, learn to rejoice!

The Bible says a cheerful heart has a continual feast. God is alive! If you understand the power of the Holy Spirit, there is no limit to what you can be and do. You can choose to have a vision for either the future or a continual nightmare. Choose God's vision, and get over what is bothering you!

CHAPTER EIGHT

Let God Anoint You for the Impossible

When circumstances are difficult and finances are short and people are sharp-tongued, look to Jesus for anointing.

A lot of people are talking about the anointing these days, and many Christians are seeking it wholeheartedly. They read books about it, they go to conferences, and they pray. They know the anointing is important, and they are willing to do whatever it takes to receive it.

Indeed, the anointing is important. In fact, it is vital. Why? Because God's anointing destroys the yoke that keeps people in bondage. It cancels the effect of sin in the lives of individuals. It frees families from fear and anger. It turns victims into overcomers. The anointing releases God's power in communities, cities, and nations. It lifts the burden from your shoulders, as well as those of your neighbors next door, and from kings and presidents and prime ministers.

The anointing forces sin to loosen its grip and nullifies its impact. The anointing changes lives through the blessed power of the Holy

Spirit. Isaiah 10:27 says, *"And it shall come to pass in that day, that his burden shall be taken away from off thy shoulder, and his yoke from off thy neck, and the yoke shall be destroyed because of the anointing."*

As a Christian, you are commanded to walk as a king and a high priest, but you cannot fulfill that call if you are in bondage to fear. God wants you be *free* from the constraints of intimidation, *free* from a life of worry and despair! You *can* rule and reign in *this* life, in the name of Jesus!

God's anointing will break the yoke that prevents your moving ahead. It *will* set you free. The anointing is absolutely essential for you to minister effectively, and the good news is that God wants you to receive His anointing more than you want it for yourself!

You Are Anointed

So why aren't more Christians experiencing the anointing? Because somewhere down the line, they got the idea that the anointing is a *thing*. They confused it with a manifestation or an emotional high. They wanted to *feel* the anointing rather than *live* it. God's anointing cannot be confined to four walls. It can't be manufactured in the pulpit, or packaged in neat little programs, or sold to the highest bidder. It is a *gift* from a loving and sovereign Father.

The fact is, if you are a child of God, you *are* anointed. Your anointing is in Jesus, and the more you relate to Him, the more it will be released in your life.

You must allow God the freedom to come to you in any way He deems appropriate. You must allow Him to release His glory and beauty and power in your life. You must allow Him to be as creative as He likes to be.

He *wants* to manifest Himself in *you* and touch the nations of the world, shaking cities and changing lives.

"Say What I Say"

The anointing within you will break every yoke and burden. All the prophets whom God called in the Bible had the anointing. Every priest had it and so did every king, and my Bible declares Jesus is a prophet, a priest, and a king.

If you want to release the anointing, allow Jesus to "live big" in you. One day I asked God for a greater anointing. Then Jesus said something that really touched me, "You will have it if you will say what I say." I thought, "Well, that shouldn't be too hard."

He also said, "You must hear what I hear." Now that is a little harder. You can say what Jesus says, but you have to guard your ears to start hearing what He hears. For instance, He does not listen to judgmental spirits. He does not listen to gossip. He does not listen to trashy music, television, or movie dialogues. Jesus does not hear those things.

Then He added one more point, "If you will say what I say, and hear what I hear, then you will do what I do." At first, I thought that would be easy, especially when I was saying what Jesus says and hearing what He hears. But, I have discovered it's not so easy. In fact, sometimes it is downright hard—but it works.

Those three commands from the Lord changed my life, "Say what I say, hear what I hear—then you'll do what I do."

Hear God

How do you begin to say what Jesus says? First, you must learn to hear God. You must be in the Word and listen with your heart. Then, when He speaks, you will know His voice. His nature and character will be familiar because of the Word, and so you will not be deceived.

Abiding in the Word will help you guard your mind and heart. This is critical if you want to avoid deception. Stay in the Word, and you will expose lying spirits who whisper in your ear! The Bible says Satan is the father of lies, and he is your soul's greatest enemy.

I could spend hours telling about the lies he has told me. I know what it is to be lied to year after year by the devil himself. His job is to distract and deceive God's people, and he will use every trick he can to keep *you* from hearing God clearly. Be alert! Guard your mind, your heart, your eyes, and your ears!

As you learn to hear the voice of God, you will notice that He speaks in a variety of ways. He is not limited to any particular method or style. Sometimes the Lord speaks through His Word. Sometimes He speaks through godly men and women. Sometimes He speaks through circumstances. Sometimes, He speaks directly to your spirit.

As you learn to hear God, and obey His Word, you allow Jesus to "live big" in your life. Then, there is a wonderful release of the anointing through the Holy Ghost. You *know* He is alive in you. Your heart is tender toward the things of the Spirit, and your prayers and ministry are effective.

I have sensed the Lord reaching out, weeping for lost and hurting souls, and touching them through me. Knowing God has spoken changes your attitude and your personality. It makes you feel differently about yourself and about other people. It makes you forgive and love and do dynamic things—even believe in the impossible.

Accomplishing the Impossible

One day I said, "I'm going to the Kremlin to preach," and somebody told me I could not. I asked, "Why not?"

"It's impossible," they said, and I replied, "Oh, thank God. I wouldn't want to go if it was possible."

I do not need God to accomplish the possible. I do not need the help and ministry of angels to do what everyone can do. I do not need a Holy Ghost arsenal for the things that are possible in life. I do not need anointing for the possible—I need it for the *impossible*.

A few short weeks later, there we were, sitting in the Kremlin Palace, a wonderful place to be. Seven thousand people packed it, and several thousand more were turned away.

When I got up to speak, they shut off my microphone, and they turned the lights off. Do you know what? The audio and lights somehow were turned back on. Many of the Soviet Supreme Council members came to our meeting. That night, I ended the service by asking how many people wanted to receive Jesus. And do you know what? Everyone in the whole palace stood.

God said the anointing would break the yoke on nations and their people. It will lift all of the burdens. The anointing will pull down all fortresses in the name of Jesus.

God told me He would give me anointing for the impossible. You *can* be happy in this world. You do not have to live a fearful, defeated existence. When circumstances are difficult, finances are short, and people are sharp-tongued, look to Jesus for the anointing.

Confidence in a Living Jesus

Do you feel the world is constantly telling you to give up? "You don't have what it takes, so forget about your dreams. You have to have potential, and kid...frankly, you don't have much."

From my earliest days of childhood, I had a very rare neurological disease, which no one could diagnose until a few years ago. I was told that it was an emotional problem, and it affected me adversely in many ways.

The devil hit me with lies repeatedly, but he never did succeed in getting me to believe them. He said, "You will never be able to look people in the face because you are weak. You came from a bad background, and you have a lot of emotional baggage. You won't ever have any confidence."

Well, he was half-right—I have learned not to have confidence in myself! When I realized I did not *have* to have confidence in my flesh, I became a desperate, dying man. I died to self in order to have the life of Jesus manifested in me.

When God gets ready to move in your life, no man can organize it and no demon can stop it. You just have to get out of the way and receive the ministry of the Holy Ghost. When you do that, you will release an anointing for the impossible.

When doctors finally diagnosed the neurological disease I had, I underwent nine hours of surgery. When I woke up in the recovery room, the devil said, "I've got you. You will never be well. You will be crippled for the rest of your life."

Don't Get Mad—Get Even

One week after the surgery, I got angry with the devil. I was supposed to be home recovering, but I was still in the hospital, and the devil was still taunting me. I turned on the television and heard that the Persian Gulf War was just about to break out.

I began praying. I told the Lord that the devil was still harassing me with his lies. The Lord said, "Why don't you do something about it? Don't get mad at the devil—get even."

"How?" I asked. "Go preach in Saudi Arabia," He replied.

I said, "Lord, first of all, I just had surgery a week ago. Second, I am Jewish, and they do not like Jews in Saudi Arabia. Third, preachers cannot go there. I read in the newspaper that no visas are being given. Even the entertainers can't go."

The Lord said, "Why do you believe the newspapers? You haven't even tried for a visa. Apply for one." So I applied, and seven days later, there it was.

Then I told the Lord my other problem: I had no invitation. It was not as if there was a Charismatic church over there sponsoring my crusades. I did not know anyone in Saudi Arabia—but God did.

I jumped on a plane and off I went, a stranger into a strange land. When the plane landed, I did not know where to go or what to do. I finally got myself to a hotel, and I said, "Father, here I am."

"Here I am," he answered.

He told me to go to the Dhahran Hotel, so I headed that way. Was I ever happy when I got there and saw huge signs saying, "Joint Operation Command." It was also headquarters for all the networks broadcasting live.

I thought, *this is great. I am going to go right in there and find the good old US of A.* I walked in with my Bible in my hand and asked, "How are you doing?"

"Who are you?" they asked.

I told them I was an evangelist, and they said, "You can't be! What are you doing with that Bible?"

Going to Jail

I did not know at the time that all chaplains had to take off their crosses. They were not even permitted to call themselves chaplains. They had to call themselves "Recreational and Motivational Coordinators."

The officials then said, "You are going to jail."

"Why?" I asked.

'You don't have a visa,' they answered. I told them I did indeed have a visa, but they did not believe me. "That's impossible," they said.

"I know," I replied with a smile. I showed them my visa, and they asked me how I got it. I told them I simply applied.

"That's impossible!" they said again.

"I know", I answered again.

"How did you get here?" they asked.

"British Airlines," I said. "They fly three times a week."

"Well, you are going to jail," they said—again.

I began to think they were right and that maybe jail would be my place of ministry, just like Paul. They told me to get my stuff, check out, and get on a plane within 4 hours, or I would be put in jail.

I walked out and got a cab, praying in the Spirit. As I was praying, I told the cab driver which way to go. I did not know that all the Air Force bases were camouflaged. The 82nd Airborne was using the Mc-Donnell Douglas aircraft plant, but they were actually meeting behind it. I walked right up to the front gate.

The sentry opened the gate and asked, "Who are you?"

"I am an evangelist."

"How did you get here?" he asked.

"British Airlines," I answered.

"That's impossible!"

"No," I replied, "They fly three times a week."

"You're going to jail," he told me.

"I know," I said. "I have already been told that, and yes, I do have a visa."

"That's impossible," he replied.

"I know," I answered. "Open the gate."

The guards opened the gate, and I walked right up to the chaplain. He said, "I don't know how in the world you got into this country. What do you want?"

"I want to preach to the troops."

He said, "I will get them all together. Then I am splitting!"

I went all over Saudi Arabia preaching to the troops in the name of Jesus. Praise God!

"You Shall Go with Me"

Without a release of the anointing, everything is impossible. However, with the anointing, you can do what God calls you to do—even those things that seem impossible!

I was humbled and encouraged to know God was using me to touch the hearts of men there in Saudi Arabia. One day, I saw some troops gathering down by the port, and I decided to have a street meeting. I just opened up my Bible and began preaching. Suddenly, a precious black brother came up to me and said, "You having church? Well, you need a song."

He opened his mouth and started singing "Amazing Grace." Man, could he sing! The others all just started gathering in. Then they started giving testimonies.

That night, the devil kept saying, "You are going to jail. You are going to jail. You had better go home." But the devil is a liar.

As I prayed that night, the Holy Spirit told me to go back to the Dhahran Hotel the next morning and ask the first person I saw if I could go with him. I thought for sure I was going to jail.

I did just as the Lord told me. "Do you mind if I go with you?" I approached a stranger and asked.

The man said, "What?"

"May I go with you?" I repeated.

"I am very angry about this. What is your name?" he asked.

"Mike Evans," I said.

"Where are you from?"

"America."

"Alright," he said, "Be here tomorrow at 6:05 a.m., and you shall go with me."

I thanked him and went on. I had never met the man in my life. I did not know where we were going. He was an Arab, and the trip ahead was getting scarier and scarier.

I showed up early the next morning. My escort met me on time, not in one vehicle, but in 15 of them, all military vehicles. He was dressed in a military uniform—he was the Commander-in-Chief of the Saudi Royal Air Force!

He put me next to him and said, "We have a secret mission on the border of Kuwait in which I will inform the Egyptian 3rd Army in the Syrian Divisions that the war will begin quickly. I am very angry because no one is supposed to know about our secret mission, but obviously, you do. Therefore, you must go. I cannot leave you behind."

"Are you a prophet?" he asked me.

"No," I replied, "I am not a prophet."

He said, "We have a very long helicopter ride, then a plane ride. You may as well relax."

As I sat next to him, I started talking about the virgin birth of Jesus and His miracles. He stopped me and said, "I like you!"

I said, "I'm glad. You did not yesterday. Why is it you like me now?" He said, "You do something for which we cut heads off and you are not afraid. Do you want to see where we do that?"

"No," I replied.

Preaching to Generals

I went on telling him about Jesus, and how He changes lives. We landed and got off the plane. The officer was there to inspect the Egyptian 3rd Army, a total of 32,000 troops. I was standing right next to him. The men first saluted him, and then they saluted me.

I said, "Your belt looks good." I figured they could not understand me anyway. Then, I said, "You have dirt on your shoes, dude." I was having a good time.

Lunchtime came, and the General was meeting in a tent with all of the generals of the Egyptian 3rd Army. He turned to me and said, "You will join me for this big meal."

At the end of the meal, he said, "They would like to know who you are."

I said, "How long can I introduce myself?"

He said, "Five minutes."

"Can I take ten, maybe?" I asked.

He said, "Not more than ten, but closer to five. I will translate."

There I was, a Jewish boy, saved and baptized in the Holy Ghost, in Saudi Arabia with a Saudi general interpreting, preaching the Gospel to the generals of the Egyptian 3rd Army. Praise God for the anointing! I could have been at home, lying in my bed feeling sick and sorry for myself.

After the General was finished there, he asked me, "What do you want to do now?" I told him I wanted to preach to the Special Forces closest to the border.

He said, "For that we need the French Foreign Legion helicopters." He called one in on his walkie-talkie. They put me on it and called ahead, announcing that they were flying in a special guest.

A Promise from a Prince

When I got back to the hotel that night, I was a walking dust bowl. The Kuwaiti royal family was there in the hotel. I was trying to get to my room to wash up when I heard a Kuwaiti prince say, "I know you. You are a friend of Yasser Arafat."

Two years before, the Lord had told me to go to Geneva and minister to Arafat. I was at the 43rd General Assembly of the United Nations and was able to stand and speak for the Lord. Arafat began screaming: "Shut up, shut up." The devil was telling me that they were going to kill me, but I was able to walk right out.

Those princes walked up to me and asked, "Are you a prophet?"

"No, I am not," I answered.

They asked, "Is God telling you something for us?"

"Yes, He is," I said. "The war will be short with hardly any bloodshed. You will have your country back quickly, but you must give the glory to Jesus."

"If this prophecy comes to pass, you shall be a guest to the royal family, and you shall come and preach about your Jesus and His cross," they said.

Do not tell me that God cannot open mighty doors! Do not tell me it is impossible!

There is a creative dynamic in the Holy Spirit like a nuclear atom. It will burst forth in the soul of a man who releases everything to God.

"I Am the Prince of Peace"

Do you remember the Madrid Peace Conference? I was able to speak 16 times. There were 5,600 press associations and 15,000 security forces there. Nobody got into the Royal Palace except officials and ministers of governments.

Yet, God told me to go. He said, "This is a peace conference, and I am the Prince of Peace."

I jumped on a plane with a doctor friend. I told him to be prepared to run fast, because we did not have an invitation. We did not—but Jesus did. We planned to go in every door that Jesus did.

When we arrived, we discovered that in two hours the first meeting was scheduled to take place with the Israelis. The person who would speak was a man whom I personally had led to the Lord nine years before. He looked at me and invited me to join him on the stage. When he finished, he handed me the microphone. I started speaking, and it was uplinked to the whole nation of Israel.

I turned to the man and asked, "What is going on next?"

He said, "Gorbachev and Shamir are meeting in the Russian Embassy in 35 minutes." I had not even gotten my bags out of the cab.

I said to my doctor friend, "Bob, we are going to the Russian Embassy. Jesus wants to be there." I told the cab driver I would pay him extra for speeding! We got there, and I ran as fast as I could up to a big black gate that was about 16 feet high. I did not see anyone behind the gate, and I realized I was at the wrong entrance.

I ran all the way around the Russian Embassy to the right gate, and found the communist press with all their credentials, screaming in Russian at Gorbachev's man. They wanted him to let them in so they could cover the meeting for the Russian government. It was five minutes until the meeting was to begin. I asked God what to do.

Credentials of the Kingdom

I remember hearing God speak to my spirit. He said, "This is my Bible. I am what it says I am." I grabbed hold of my Bible and said, "You. Come here. I want in."

He said, "You want in? Where are your credentials?" I held up my Bible.

He turned and started walking away. I told him to come back. He was about three steps away when he turned. I pointed my finger at him and said, "In the name of Jesus, open the gate and let me in."

That man pushed a button and pulled me through that gate. Tears were streaming down my face. I thought, "Oh Lord, I can't cry now."

I was right in the room with Shamir and Gorbachev, and the Russian press were on the outside! What happened the rest of the week? I was in the Royal Palace for every session; I was the only minister in the world allowed in the Royal Palace at that moment.

No one understood how I got in. I was able to speak again, again, and again. I was uplinked live with Secretary of State James Baker with my Bible, giving the Word of the Lord as the event was covered globally.

Ministers of states and countries all over the world came up to me and asked, "Are you a minister?"

"Yes, I am," I said.

"What country?" they asked.

"Not a country," I said. "But a kingdom—the kingdom of God."

They would say, "You don't look Arab."

No, I don't. I hope I look like Jesus. Full of grace, truth, and wisdom—God did all this to glorify His Son. He opened door after door after door—and only He really knows all the lives that were forever changed in Madrid that week.

Rain in the Desert

God told me to give Him 20 years and touch the nations of the world. So, I went to Uganda. We were there in a huge Moslem soccer field. I was filled with anticipation and I thought: "Boy, now it is going to happen. God is going to show up and begin to touch the nations of the world!"

We had the worst rainstorm I had ever seen in my life just 30 minutes before our meeting was to start. Fifty people ended up standing in the rain. The only reason they did not leave was that they were all crippled or blind.

I looked at that mud hole, and I said, "God, this isn't Your will.

He whispered, "Son, it is. Preach."

I was reminded of a sermon Oral Roberts preached years ago, called "It Is Going to Rain on Your Desert." I did not remember the sermon, but I remembered the title!

The third night, I was standing before 200,000 people holding my Bible up and saying, "The Word of God is the power of God unto salvation." I have declared that truth hundreds of times, but never in my life have I seen a response like the one I saw that night. Everyone in the field started shaking.

I was afraid to put the Bible down. I did not know what to do. These were not Pentecostals—they were Muslims. A train was coming down the track behind us, and I thought that perhaps it was the train was causing all the shaking. The conductor stopped the train and came running out of it. Others followed and ran into the field where they, too, began shaking.

Suddenly, I saw the most beautiful sight. Africans who were wearing demonic fetishes started taking them off and placing them in a pile in the center of the field. They burned their objects of demonic worship and denounced the power of witchcraft!

God is ready, ready, ready to do great things!

A Healing in El Salvador

Another time, God told me to go to El Salvador. I had only 31 days to plan an entire crusade. I said, "God, it takes a *year* to plan a crusade." But, there's no point in arguing with God. He is in charge, and you must submit your will to His, your plans to His, your schedule to His. He knows what He is doing.

I told a number of church leaders what I intended to do, and gave them the time constraints God had given me. They told me they thought I was out of the will of God. "It is impossible," they said.

I said, "Oh, good! That is a confirmation." Then, they informed me that the last person who tried to pull a crusade together in the blink of an eye failed miserably.

Thirty-one days later, I was in El Salvador, speaking on a television program. Little did I know that the director and host would be saved and turn the program over to me. It became like *The 700 Club* as people started calling in, accepting Jesus, and getting healed.

I was able to meet with the President of El Salvador and talk to him about the healing of his nation. I read Second Chronicles 7:14 to him, which says, *"If my people, which are called by my name, shall humble themselves, and pray, and seek my face, and turn from their wicked ways; then will I hear from heaven, and will forgive their sin, and will heal their land."*

The Vice President's wife called and asked me to come and pray for her. As I headed toward the palace, we passed through the center of town and saw an old, dirty, crippled man. The Holy Ghost told me to stop and pray for him. I said I would, but figured I would catch him later.

I drove all the way up to the palace. God told me He was not going in that palace. He said, "I told you to pray for that crippled man. I want you to do it *now*. You go and pray for him, and then come back here."

I waved and said I would be back. I did not have time to explain. I just had the car turn and go to that man. I knew I was in the perfect will of God, and the anointing would be there. I laid my hands on him, and he threw down his crutches; he was gloriously healed by the power of God.

A Vision of Jesus

When we went to Madras, India, my daughter, Shira, went with us. In my hotel that night, I saw a vision of Jesus. I had not seen anything like it since the Lord appeared to me in my room when I was 11 years old.

In the vision, I saw idols. I thought they were the Indian idols. The Lord asked me whose they were. I told Him, "They are idols of India."

He said, "No, Mike, they are yours."

I looked at one of the idols, and it said "pride." Another said "selfishness." When I awoke, I thought I was going to die. I felt like the life was being crushed out of me because of God's holiness. I fell on the floor and began praying. As I poured out my heart in repentance, the Holy Ghost began cleansing me. Then, He filled me and anointed me so He could do what He wanted to do.

It may not be big stuff to everyone, but when God wants to shake a nation, nothing can stand in His way. Fifteen minutes later, my daughter was there on her face before the Lord. The whole crusade team ended up on the floor that night, pouring out their hearts before the Lord.

Did God move in Madras? Yes, in a crusade that wasn't supposed to happen. The crowds lined up for miles to greet me. We were told we preached to over one million people. One man said he believed many Muslims and Hindus came to Christ in those five nights.

God is in the miracle-working business. Jesus is here, and He is alive. What is between you and your miracle? Nothing but Jesus.

As that beautiful song says, "Fill my cup, Lord, fill it up. Come and quench this thirsting in my soul. Bread of heaven, feed me till I want no more. Fill my cup. Fill it up and make me whole."

When *God* puts a thirsting in your soul, you will have a different attitude. When He makes you hunger for Him, you will be changed. Matthew 5:6 says, *"Blessed are they which do hunger and thirst after righteousness: for they shall be filled."*

Be blessed today! God has placed within your heart an anointing that will break the yoke and set you free. He has anointed you to minister love and healing to others. He has anointed you to do the impossible in the name of Jesus and the power of the Holy Ghost! Go— and bless others!

CHAPTER NINE

Defeat Your Enemy

*Draw near. Get into that place of anointing where the
glory of God is, where the sick are healed and captives
are set free.*

Joshua was Moses' replacement. He had his hands full: he was trying to lead a nation, build an army, overthrow Israel's adversaries
and conquer new territory. After his inauguration as leader, God
visited Joshua, bringing him hope, encouragement and peace of
mind. Instantly, Joshua developed a strong relationship with the God
of Israel, yielding to His directives and commands.

This deep Divine connection carried over to Joshua's leadership
skills, by which he instilled his beliefs and convictions into his committed soldiers. The Bible says, *"And it came to pass, when they
brought out those kings unto Joshua, that Joshua called for all the men
of Israel, and said unto the captains of the men of war which went with
him, Come mar, put your feet upon the necks of these kings. And they
came near, and put their feet upon the necks of them. And Joshua said
unto them, Fear not, nor be dismayed, be strong and of good courage:
for thus shall the Lord do to all your enemies against whom ye fight"*

(Joshua 10:24-25).

Joshua told his men of war to "come near." The word "*near*" in Hebrew is *nagosh,* a verb that has several definitions. One meaning is "to approach." It carries the idea, "to leave your gods which cannot save you and approach God or draw near, as to the Holy of Holies." This is the meaning used in Numbers 4:19 and Exodus 30:20.

Nagosh and Worship

When the Scripture talks about approaching as you would approach the Holy of Holies, God is issuing a command, not making a request. *Nagosh* is an action verb. It is coming near and worshipping God in high praise. Worshipping is seeking God in the spirit, glorifying Him, magnifying Him, allowing Him to lift us into the heavenlies.

Another meaning of this verb is "to offer or present." When you approach the Lord in worship, you must have a heart that is soft and responsive to His Spirit. You must be pliable, ready to listen, willing to obey. This verb also means "to move from one place to another" or "to move out of a place of hardness into a place of tenderness with God."

Draw near to the Lord! Get into that place of high praise, that place of anointing where the glory of God is, where the sick are healed and captives are set free. When you draw near, wonderful things begin to happen. When you refuse to draw near, what happens? The enemy rules and reigns in your life. You become full of fear and in bondage to sin. But, it doesn't have to be that way! You can put your foot on the Enemy's neck!

The Lion's Roar

The Bible says Satan comes as a roaring lion. The lions I am talking about are not animals but evil spirits, they roar when they have captured their prey and they "roar" through people. The old lions roar to scare you, and the young lions roar to capture you. When they take you captive, they are boasting.

The Enemy attempts to take Christians captive. When the Enemy captures you and you refuse to draw near to God, you will not get released. You allow the Enemy to intimidate you, and in so doing, you are controlled by him.

But, there is a way to draw near to God and be set free. Second Corinthians 11:2-3 says, *"For I am jealous over you with godly jealousy: for I have espoused you to one husband, that I may present you as a chaste virgin to Christ. But I fear; lest by any means, as the serpent beguiled Eve through his subtlety, so your minds should be corrupted from the simplicity that is in Christ."*

Get Ready to Fight

Joshua recognized that the kings had complete authority and power over the people. He knew something had to be done if the people were to be freed, so he went to his captains of war. He gave them new orders—they had to put their feet on the enemy's neck.

In Luke 14:31-32, the Bible talks about the cost of war. What does war bring to the Christian? It brings affliction and persecution, along with blessing. God says He will bless you, but you will experience persecution. You will be attacked, especially if you are doing God's work. The devil will use unbelievers and carnal Christians to discourage you. He will whisper lies in your ear when you are tired and alone. He will try to steal the Word of God from your heart. He will do whatever he can to bring confusion and fear into your life—and get your eyes off Jesus and on your problems. But the Lord says He will fight the battle with you—and you will prevail.

I am appalled when I see the condition of the Church today, and when I realize the pressure the family is under. I do not see an abundance of joy or love. People are preoccupied with so many things.

Instead of seeing healthy relationships, I see fear, manipulation, judgment, anger, and distractions. That is the work of the enemy. He is trying to rob us of the power and authority that is ours through Jesus Christ.

Become an Obstacle

The Bible tells us in First Peter to love one another. It also says you must humble yourself in God's hand so that He may raise you up. Why? Because the Enemy prowls about as a roaring lion seeking someone whom he can devour.

The prophet Isaiah warned that some people would even become a "smooth road" for the enemy to walk on! But you do not have to be a smooth road! You need to become an obstacle to the enemy—a huge obstacle, in Jesus' name! God will give you the grace and strength to resist the Enemy.

Ephesians 6 tells us to put on the armor of God so you can withstand the devil. You have a mighty weapon at your disposal: the Word of God. Ephesians 6 calls it "the sword of the Spirit." Read the Word. Believe it. Meditate on its truths. Let it speak to you. Then speak the Word to others. Pray the Word. Let it permeate every part of your life. Use the weapon God has given you to defeat the Enemy!

Are you making use of the shield of faith, the helmet of salvation, and the breastplate of righteousness? The Word of God works! Remember, you are not wrestling against mere flesh and blood but against principalities and powers of darkness.

In 1979, when our ministry offices were in New York, I was tormented by fear. Some members of the Jewish community had sent us death threats. They had destroyed our property and harassed us. The Enemy tried to distract me with fear and intimidation. It worked. I had on my sword and my shield, but I was so scared I ended up in the intensive care unit of the local hospital. I knew I was not supposed to have that fear, but I did.

I was afraid of someone knowing that I was afraid! That is not Christianity—that is sickness. I did not know that preachers could be in bondage. I did not know I could be released from fear.

Know the Enemy

Another important word that we see in Joshua 10:24-25 is "enemy" or, in Hebrew, "*tsarar*" It means, "to bind or roll in a bundle, like rocks in your path." The Enemy wants to put rocks in your path.

In Deuteronomy 11:16, Moses told the children of Israel to take heed lest their hearts be deceived. The Hebrew word for "deceived" is "*patha*" and it means "deceit" or "to expand your mind." In other words, when you are deceived, you spread out your thinking so the Seducer can do his ugly work in you.

When you are not grounded in the Word, you are susceptible to deception and defeat. You are not able to put your foot on the devil's neck. You are easily offended. You operate in the fleshly realm rather than the spiritual. You are preoccupied. You judge others. You are critical. You are full of fear and unbelief. You have no joy because you are fighting people instead of your real enemy—the devil!

Jesus said Satan comes only to kill, steal, and destroy—but He came to give us abundant life!

Do what Joshua told his men of war to do, draw near to God! Do not be afraid. And put your feet on the neck of the Enemy!

In order to become an overcomer, you must be sensitive to the Holy Spirit. You must walk in faith and obedience. Consider Joshua. He had the answer you need today. He gathered the captains and his men of war and said, "Let's be the army of God. Come near and put your feet on the necks of the kings. *Nagosh!* Draw near to God!"

CHAPTER TEN

Seek Power in Persecution

*God's anointing does not come from doing—it comes
from being.*

A friend of mine was going through a life crisis and was under a lot of pressure. He prayed, "Oh, Lord, deliver me from the battle." But the Lord responded to him by saying, "I will deliver you *into* the battle." Too many Christians fail to recognize that battles will come, and the Lord has equipped us with weapons, discernment, and the power to overcome.

In Philippians 4:13, the apostle Paul said, *"I can do all things through Christ who strengthens me."* You would think that Paul would have told us exactly what he did when he was under pressure and when he was persecuted. Most people would focus on the battle, even ramble on and on about it, but not Paul.

Attitude and Character

Paul was seemingly at the end of his life's journey when he said he could do all things through Christ. *"I can do all things through*

Christ who strengthens me," was his secret. Paul explained how he became a victorious Christian—it had to do with his attitude and character. In Philippians, he tells us how he held onto his joy, even in the face of persecution. The people were probably saying, "We have a serious problem. Everything is coming apart at the seams. Confusion abounds. All hell is breaking loose. Paul, show us what to do."

What did Paul say? Did he give them a piece of his mind? No, Paul rejoiced in the Lord.

Didn't Paul know that Demos had forsaken him? Yes, but he was not defeated by it. Philippians 4:6 says he poured his heart out to God, *"Be careful for nothing; but in everything by prayer and supplication with thanksgiving let your requests be made known unto God."*

Didn't Paul realize that the churches were in a mess? Yes, but he was not fretful because of it. He trusted the Lord, and as a result, peace reigned in the midst of trouble. Philippians 4:7 says, *"And the peace of God, which passeth all understanding, shall keep your hearts and minds through Christ Jesus."*

Don't Do—Be!

Paul was sitting in a Roman prison, and some of the churches in which God had used him greatly were now operating with dysfunctional and disobedient lifestyles. The people were guilty of all kinds of sin and false teachings—everything you could imagine.

Runners were going back and forth, telling him what was happening in the churches. One day, Nero got angry and burned down half of Rome, then blamed it on the Christians—while Paul was still in prison. Demos, a co-laborer of Paul's, took off and deserted him when the fire started.

However, through the entire book of Philippians, Paul says nothing about what he did...just that God gave him strength.

Why did he say he could do all things through Christ without telling us what those things were? Because he was focused on *attitude* not just *action*. He was describing *how* he responded, not simply what he did.

Are you trying to do something for God? If so, stop. God does not want you to *do* anything *for* Him. He wants you to *be* something in Jesus. If you will *be*, He will *do*. We already have a religious world out there trying to *do*.

Paul understood the importance of taking his thoughts captive to the obedience of Christ. He said in Philippians 4:8, *"Finally, brethren, whatsoever things are true, whatsoever things are honest, whatsoever things are just, whatsoever things are pure, whatsoever things are lovely, whatsoever things are of good report; if there be any virtue, and if there be any praise, think on these things."* What a statement for a man in prison to make! He had such a tremendous anointing on him; indeed, the anointing helped birth the Church.

Paul was saying to be content in any situation. Most people do not see that for what it is, a requirement for living as a victorious, anointed person of God. Many Christians want the growth process to be trouble-free. They want to be able to please God by doing the right things. The Bible makes it clear that God looks at the heart first. Actions are important, but He also examines our motives. Why? Because actions are simply expressions of what is already in the heart. I will say it again, the anointed life does not come from *doing*—it comes from *being*.

Paul did not lose his peace, joy, confidence, or willingness to forgive because of persecution. How did he develop this kind of strength? Let us take a closer look at him.

To begin with, before his conversion to Christianity, Paul was a murderer. He had been the number one man whom the chief priest trusted to persecute the Church. He killed the saints, or consigned them to death. He chased them into prison, and voted against them.

The Bible says that one day Jesus appeared to Paul and said, "You are persecuting *Me*." That was a revelation to Paul—and it is significant for you as well. If you are being persecuted as a Christian, remember the persecution is directed at *Christ* and not you. That means the battles you fight are not yours if you are in Christ—they are the Lord's.

Paul's Ministry Begins

Knocked off his horse and struck blind for three days, Paul sat in a dark room with no food or anything else to comfort him. Then, the Holy Ghost touched a man by the name of Ananias, and he went to Paul and laid hands on him. Paul was instantly healed.

After that, Galatians 1:11-18 says that Paul went to Arabia where he allowed God to develop his character. He learned to listen to the Lord and walk in His truth. Then Barnabas came and recruited Paul and his ministry for preaching began. Acts 9 says he proclaimed Jesus in Syria—and right away, he was persecuted for it. In fact, there was a plot to kill him.

From there, Paul went to Jerusalem to talk to the disciples. He knocked on their door, but at first, they would not let him in because he was known as the greatest persecutor of Christians. They were afraid of him. They did not believe his claim to salvation was real until Barnabas explained what had happened to Paul.

Later, he took Silas and went to Philippi to preach the gospel. But, the people tore off his clothes, beat him, and threw him in prison.

What would you do if you were Paul? Take legal action against someone? Put your foot down and get an attorney? Didn't they know who he was?

Demons Knew Him

They did know who Paul was—that is, the demons knew. That is why they declared, "Paul, we know." They knew who he was, all right, but Paul was not intimidated by demons and their spiritual attacks. He did not operate in the flesh. He did not get angry and demand his rights. He gave his problems to the Lord.

A man who shook his fist at the crowd did not occupy the cross of Jesus Christ. It held a Man who willingly suffered the humiliation, the beatings, and the rejection for our sake. In the face of death, Jesus said, "Father forgive them for they don't know what they are doing."

In Acts 16, Paul and Silas had been beaten and thrown into a dark prison cell, and still they said, "Let's sing to the Lord." When they began to praise the Lord, the prisoners heard them. The jailer was so impacted that he and his entire family gave their hearts to Jesus!

"My Mother is Dead"

Many people are spiritual prisoners today, and they are hurting. My mother was like that. Before she died, the devil said, "I will kill her, and she will deny Jesus"—and she did. I flew to her house, and one of my sisters and brothers tried to have the service before I got there. Then they took her money.

I had been paying her house and car payments for five years. They spent the money on themselves for booze and drugs and one of them bought a car. When I got to the house, I saw a group of drugged people, having a beer party.

My mother's body was at the funeral home. They did not want to bury her because they did not want to spend the money. The night she died, my father had asked her for a divorce. He told her he did not love her anymore and left her. She had a bad heart and was not supposed to be upset.

I walked into to the room, where at the age of eleven, I had seen Jesus. I got down on my knees and said, "Jesus, in this room, You appeared to me as I cried all night. You told me You loved me. God, my mother is dead, what are You going to do?"

He brought two Scriptures to mind instantly. The first was Second Timothy 1:7, which says, *"I have not given you a spirit of fear, but of power, love and a sound mind."* Then He reminded me of the verse that says He will direct our steps. He promised He would redeem the situation.

Then, God said, "Mike, who killed your mother? Who is causing all the problems right now?" Instantly, everything came into focus. I knew who the Enemy was, and I knew what had to be done.

I could have done many things when the devil killed my mother. I could have beaten my brothers. I could have cursed them for their selfishness. Or, I could have joined them in their revelry. I could have turned my back on God. But I didn't. I chose to believe that God had not given me a spirit of fear, but of power, love and a sound mind. I chose to believe He would direct my steps as He said He would and redeem the situation.

My older brother was high when I approached him. I looked him straight in the eyes and said, "You will be saved. I am coming for you."

I looked at the whole family, at my sister who had been a prostitute for twenty years and was teaching reincarnation. I looked at my brother who was involved in organized crime.

I said to each of them, "You will be depressed and discouraged. You will worry, but I won't, because I am not going to get angry. I am going after the one who killed our mother, and I am taking 10,000 of his in place of the one he took from me."

Go After the Devil

That was Paul's response to persecution, too. You can hear bad reports, then sit around and gossip, or get angry and take sides—and still get nowhere. Or, you can find out what—or who—is really causing the problem and go after *him*.

Do not let the devil jerk you around! Go after him! Paul did.

I was speaking at a meeting outside Washington, D.C., sometime after my mother died. There were over 23,000 people attending. Between January of that year and the time of the meeting in Washington, I had seen over 8,000 people saved. I said, "God, I asked You to let me see souls come to Jesus. Will You honor that prayer?"

When I gave people the opportunity to give their hearts to Jesus, I specifically asked for homosexuals, fornicators, drug addicts, alcoholics and prostitutes to come forward. Over 2,000 people responded!

I stopped right in the middle of the altar call and said, "Devil, remember! Remember when you killed my mother? Remember what I told you? Devil, there they are! God has given me 10,000 of your souls for the one you have taken!" Did my plan work? Did I take 10,000 souls from the devil, in the name of Jesus? Yes!

What was Paul's response to persecution? He was a mighty man of miracles, a man of healing, and a man of faith. Yet, he was still persecuted and thrown into prison. It seemed that everything was at stake.

Paul knew differently. Nothing was really at stake because he had nothing left—everything he *had* and everything he *was* belonged to the Lord. He did not need to defend himself. He knew that Jesus is the solid Rock. He is your Refuge, and you can depend on Him—no matter what your circumstances look like.

What will your response be to pressure and persecution? Do not give up your joy. Do not give in to fear. Rejoice in the Lord and you will find power in persecution!

CHAPTER ELEVEN

Conquer Vain Imaginations

The life of Jesus will destroy darkness in your heart—
darkness which creates evil, vain imaginations.

Have you ever been up at 4:00 AM., when it is still dark? Perhaps you are one of those who likes to see the sunrise. When I hunt, I get up about 4:00 in the morning, and I usually take time to pray. At about 5:30 or 6:00, the sun starts coming up.

When I am in my deer stand, in the dark, it is easy to start imagining things. Trees and stumps begin to look like deer and other animals. If I allow it, I can imagine all sorts of things out there.

When you are in a place that is dark spiritually, your thoughts can run wild, and fear can grip your heart. God does not want you to allow that to happen! He wants you to tear down imaginations and bring every thought captive! Consider Second Corinthians 10:4-5 where it says, *"For the weapons of our warfare are not carnal, but mighty through God to the pulling down of strong holds; Casting down imaginations and every high thing that exalteth itself against the knowledge of God, and bringing into captivity every thought to the obedience of Christ."*

Indeed, certain things happen when you are in spiritual darkness. Vain imaginations grow and thrive, but in the light, they are all wiped away. You cannot conquer vain imaginations with anything but light.

Light on the Holy Mount

Matthew describes an amazing experience that Peter, James, and John had when they were with Jesus. They had all climbed up a high mountain far from the pressing crowds when suddenly, the disciples saw Jesus change physically, right in front of their eyes. *"And was transfigured before them: and his face did shine as the sun, and his raiment was white as the light."* (17:2). There He stood, talking with Moses and Elijah! Then, they heard a voice from heaven, which said: *"This is my beloved Son, in whom I am well pleased; hear ye him."* (17:5).

Years later, Peter recalled this experience in a letter to the Church. He insisted he was not repeating mere hearsay about Jesus. No, he was certain that everything he shared was true because he saw it and heard it himself, including the transfiguration. Then, he makes an interesting application. He says you have the light of Christ shining in your heart to dispel the darkness! *"And this voice which came from heaven we heard, when we were with him in the holy mount. We have also a more sure word of prophecy; whereunto ye do well that ye take heed, as unto a light that shineth in a dark place, until the day dawn, and the day star arise in your hearts"* (2 Peter 1:18-19).

The word *"light"* here actually refers to a *"portable light."* In other words, you can take the light of Jesus with you anywhere you go, and expect to see the darkness flee.

If you want to hear God speak to you, then you must go onto the holy mount. You must get away for a while. Open the Word, and be still. Listen, and expect to hear.

Many people have Bibles, but they do not benefit from them. That is a little like having a steak dinner set before you and refusing to eat it. You can starve to death in the midst of abundance.

The reason so many Christians don't experience the power of God's Word is because they haven't walked away from the crowds and distractions and asked God to release His anointing in them.

Examine Yourself

There was no darkness that day on the holy mount. There was only the light and the glory of God. *"He that saith he is in the light, and hateth his brother, is in darkness even until now"* (1John 2:9). In other words, if you are living in darkness, you will stumble.

If you are harboring any unforgiveness in your heart, you are in the dark, and you are sure to stumble. Your brother may have offended you and treated you unjustly, but the Bible says that if you hate your brother, you are in darkness. Spiritual darkness is debilitating. You cannot see where you are going when you are in the dark. You just bump along and hope you do not fall into a pit.

That is one reason why the Bible tells you not to take communion unworthily without examining yourself. First Corinthians 11:27-30 says, *"Wherefore whosoever shall eat this bread, and drink this cup of the Lord, unworthily, shall be guilty of the body and blood of the Lord. But let a man examine himself, and so let him eat of that bread, and drink of that cup. For he that eateth and drinketh unworthily, eateth and drinketh damnation to himself, not discerning the Lord's body. For this cause many are weak and sickly among you, and many sleep."*

What does it mean to discern the Lord's body? It means you are to respect and care for one another, since the Church is the Body of Christ. It means you are to build each other up. It means you are to expel the spirit of religious judgment: Drive out the spirit of confusion! Reject fear! Banish rejection! Refuse pride! These things violate the revelation you receive from God's Word. They cloud your vision so you cannot see the light that is shining through the darkness of vain imaginations. Nurture meaningful relationships. Confront one another in love. Be there when someone is suffering. Invest your time and share your heart.

Christians Need "Summit Dialogue"

Several years ago during the summit meeting of President George H. W. Bush and President Mikhail Gorbachev, I saw something I considered very positive. In reality, Bush and Gorbachev were millions of miles apart in every aspect, but with all their differences, they were still able to sit down to communicate and negotiate.

Although I disagreed with some of their decisions, I was impressed by their persistence. I thought about the phenomenal contrast between that summit dialogue and communication within the Church. Do you realize that the world behaves more wisely than Christians in many ways?

Often, when Christians have differences, they do not communicate. They do not even disagree agreeably. They just get offended and scorn one another. First Peter 1:12 says, *"Wherefore I will not be negligent to put you always in remembrance of these things, though ye know them, and be established in the present truth."* God's marvelous revelation of truth will destroy darkness in our hearts!

God wants you to speak the truth in love, but He wants you to *speak* to your brother! When you are offended, remember what Psalm 119:165 says, *"Great peace have they which love thy law: and nothing shall offend them."* There may be times when your feelings are hurt, but that does not mean you have to be offended.

It is easy to let your mind replay the painful scene repeatedly, and imagine what you could have done differently, but that is useless! The result of such thinking is a defensive attitude and a fortified wall between you and your brother. If you give the enemy an opportunity, then he will build a strong case of why you should fear rejection and further disappointment.

You must take the initiative. Examine yourself first. Ask God to search your heart and reveal areas of pride and bitterness. Repent and ask the Spirit to fill you anew. Then, confront your brother in love as God directs. Bear in mind the goal is *restoration*, not revenge.

Seven Things God Hates

If you give them the chance, vain imaginations will exalt themselves above the Word of God. The minute you allow this to happen, you are laying your weapons aside and accepting defeat.

Proverbs 6:16-19 says there are seven things the Lord hates:

1. A proud look
2. A lying tongue
3. Hands that shed innocent blood
4. A heart that devises wicked imaginations
5. Feet that are swift in running to mischief
6. A false witness that speaks lies
7. He that sows discord among brethren

God says, "I hate these things." When God hates something, look out! When you make God mad, you have a problem! Look at the list again:

1. A proud look is an attitude that says, "I am really something. In fact, I deserve special treatment I shouldn't be serving anyone; I should be served." Proverbs 16:18 says, *"Pride goeth before destruction, and a haughty spirit before a fall."*

2. A lying tongue is a person willing to "bend the truth" for your own benefit, even if it is at the expense of someone else. Psalm 62:3-4 says, *"How long will ye imagine mischief against a man? ye shall be slain all of you: as a bowing wall shall ye be, and as a tottering fence. They only consult to cast him down from his excellency: they delight in lies: they bless with their mouth, but*

they curse inwardly. Selah."

3. Hands that shed innocent blood is an attitude of hatred, anger, and selfishness. 1 John 3:15 says, *"Whosoever hateth his brother is a murderer: and ye know that no murderer hath eternal life abiding in him."*

4. A heart that devises wicked imaginations is a refusal to harness evil thoughts, and wicked thoughts lead to wicked deeds. Proverbs 23:7 says, *"For as he thinketh in his heart, so is he... "*

5. Feet that are swift in running to mischief is an attitude that intends to satisfy the flesh quickly, at any cost. It is a thrill-seeking, dangerous, "me first" way of life. Proverbs 1:10-19 says, *"If young toughs tell you, 'Come and join us'—turn your back on them! 'We'll hide and rob and kill,' they say. 'Good or bad, we'll treat them all alike. And the loot we'll get! All kinds of stuff! Come on, throw in your lot with us; we'll split with you in equal shares.' Don't do it, son! Stay far from men like that, for crime is their way of life, and murder is their specialty. When a bird sees a trap being set, it stays away, but not these men; they trap themselves! They lay a booby trap for their own lives. Such is the fate of all who live by violence and murder. They will die a violent death."* (LB).

6. A false witness that speaks lies is a person willing to slander others, regardless of the damage it does. Proverbs 19:5, 9 says, *"A false witness shall not be unpunished, and he that speaketh lies shall not escape. A false witness shall not be unpunished, and he that speaketh lies shall perish."*

7. One that sows discord among brethren is a person who is petty, murmurs, is contentious, and has a strife-filled attitude that stirs up trouble at every opportunity. Proverbs 6:12-15 says, *"A worthless person, a wicked man, Is the one who walks with a false mouth, Who winks with his eyes, who signals with his feet, Who points with his fingers; Who with perversity in his*

heart devises evil continually, Who spreads strife. Therefore his calamity will come suddenly; Instantly he will be broken, and there will be no healing." (NASB).

Notice that all of these sins begin in the mind, which is the thought of evil, followed by the intention, and resulting in the action. God says He hates these things! So should you!

Casting Down Vain Imaginations

What creates vain imaginations? Most of the time, they come through an offense. The Bible is filled with examples of godly people dealing with injustice, difficult circumstances, and various other problems—without getting offended.

Acts 7 tells the story of Stephen, his defense of the gospel, and his subsequent stoning. How in the world could Stephen keep from getting offended when his killers began to throw rocks at him? Verse 60 says, *"And he kneeled down, and cried with a loud voice, Lord, lay not this sin to their charge. And when he had said this, he fell asleep."*

Why didn't Stephen fear for his life? Why did he not get angry and strike back? Why, of all things, did he ask God to forgive the ones who were about to kill him? Simple. Because he was filled with the Holy Ghost.

When you are tempted to harbor an offense against someone, how should you respond? The first thing you must do is determine that you want to have favor with God. Your heart must be right. If God's approval is of utmost importance, then your feelings can be sorted out properly. They can be submitted to Him, and you can receive the wisdom and grace you need to forgive.

When you are offended, you become prone to gossip and form wrong opinions. Your heart has been wounded, and instead of turning to the Lord for healing, you lash out at others, creating further hurt and division. Churches experience major splits because of offenses that should have been released to the healing and restoring power of the Holy Spirit.

If you have been wounded, seek the Lord. Ask Him to heal your heart and help you to forgive. Then, reach out in love to the one who offended you! Allow God to restore you both and establish peace once again.

You Versus the Issues of Life

Proverbs 24:10 says, *"If thou faint in the day of adversity, thy strength is small."* You are living in a day of tremendous pressure and adversity— are you going to faint? The temptation to harbor an offense is greatest when you have pressures in your life. If you allow stress to determine your actions, you are walking in darkness. That kind of darkness can blind you to the truth and keep you from responding as you should. That is why you have to renew your mind.

God has to do something in your life to form His character in you. He wants you to look and act like Jesus! Sometimes He allows pressures to build as a way of refining your patience and faith. You are more important to God than the issues you face. The stress and pressures are temporary. Remember that. They will pass in time. You must be strong enough to face them as a man or woman of faith.

Jesus died so you could have abundant life. He did not die for issues or causes. He died for you. He also rose again, making you a conqueror in Him. You will overcome the pressures of life when you recognize His love and care for you, and submit to His lordship.

Hurting the Heart of God

When you permit vain imaginations to dictate your responses, you are hurting yourself. But more important, you are hurting the heart of God. Jesus died for you, that's true, but He also died for the one against whom you are holding a grudge.

When you refuse to control your thoughts and emotions, you insult the Lord. You are saying in essence, "I don't care if You shed Your blood for that individual. The bitterness I feel and the revenge I desire is more important to me than Your mercy, forgiveness, and restoration." Matthew 6:12; 14-15 says, *"And forgive us our debts, as we forgive our debtors. . . For if ye forgive men their trespasses, your heavenly Father will also forgive you: But if ye forgive not men their trespasses, neither will your Father forgive your trespasses."*

If you have been holding a grudge against someone, why not stop right now and pray with me:

"Dear Lord, I don't want to hurt You. I'm sorry I have put my own feelings above Your Word. I'm sorry I have let my imagination run rampant. Show me the way You want me to walk. Give me a heart of forgiveness and restoration. Show me how I can have an attitude of gratitude. In Jesus' name, Amen."

CHAPTER TWELVE

Learn from Adversity

*You will regain strength from adversity if you humble
yourself, face your problems, rebuke the enemy, bless
God, and do His will.*

Texas is a place that gets an abundance of cold, north winds as well as warm, southerly winds. On one occasion, I remember how warm it was when I entered an office in Dallas and how bitter it was when I left. The temperature dropped from 80 degrees to 32 degrees—because of the wind! In a number of passages, the Bible speaks about the *east wind,* and it usually represents adversity. In the book of Exodus, for instance, we read that God caused the east wind to blow locusts into Egypt.

Everyone goes through hardships, but not everyone handles problems in a productive way. Job 27:21 says, *"The east wind carrieth him away, and he departeth: and as a storm hurleth him out of his place."* What about you? When your kids are in trouble, how do you respond? When you are under financial pressure, what course of action do you take? When there is a serious illness in your family, how do you pray? Do you get angry when adversity comes your way, or fearful? Do you face your problems squarely?

In Hosea 13:15, we read, *"Though he be fruitful among his brethren, an east wind shall come, the wind of the Lord shall come up from the wilderness, and his spring shall become dry, and his fountain shall be dried up: he shall spoil the treasure of all pleasant vessels."* Some people are unable to deal with the pressures of life so they have nervous breakdowns. Others become violent. Still others commit suicide. What about you?

Wake Up!

The first, and perhaps most important, way to deal with trouble is to wake up! Rise and face the wind of adversity. Do not just lie around and feel sorry for yourself. Many Christians would rather sleep through difficult times. They prefer to go back to bed and pull the covers over their heads. They hide from painful experiences and moan, "Woe is me. Nobody has it as tough as I do." That is foolish thinking. What's more, that approach to adversity doesn't work!

Jeremiah 25:32 says, *"Thus saith the Lord of hosts, Behold, evil shall go forth from nation to nation, and a great whirlwind shall be raised up from the coasts of the earth."* God is saying, "I want to make you like a great wind that confronts adversity. I do not want you to lie down in hard times. Arise! Face the east wind!"

Adversity is either the devil's tool of torment or God's tool that teaches you to trust. The choice is yours. The devil *wants* you to worry about your life. At night, for instance, when you go to bed, he will whisper in your ear, "You had a lot of problems to deal with today, didn't you?" Then, he will try to make you replay all those difficulties so you will focus on them and give in to worry.

When you awaken the next morning, he will repeat the process, "You've got to face all those problems again today, don't you?" he says. "It's never going to end."

You can be certain of one thing: worrying will *not* change your problems. It will *not* help you feel better. The only thing worrying does is make everything seem worse. Do not despair! If you are caught up in the east wind of adversity, there is a way out!

Pursue the Blessings of God

If you want to overcome adversity, you must get the blessings of God working in your life. Be aware, however, that blessings do not always come easily. More often than not, you will have to fight for them.

In Hebrew, the word *"barauch"* means *"to bless."* In Genesis 12:3 God said, *"I will bless them that bless thee, and curse him that curseth thee: and in thee shall all families of the earth be blessed."* If you speak even a small blessing, God will give you a big blessing.

The first time the word *"curse"* is used in this Scripture it means *"gossip."* The second time the word *"curse"* is used it means *"to give heavy blows."* In other words, if you gossip about others, God will visit you with heavy blows.

Bless people! Reverse the curse! When you are dealing with adversity, let blessing flow from your lips, and God will reward you. If you want to get out of the pressure, reverse the curse! You must not get bitter; you have to get better. In other words, you have to redirect the east wind.

Go and Do!

There are givers and takers in this world, and it is not hard to tell who gives and who takes. The givers are also good receivers. You can see it in their physical bodies, in their spirits, in their homes, and in their work. They know how to receive from God. They have released a spirit of giving. They readily offer their time, their abilities, and their money. They are obedient to the Lord and as a result, God blesses them. You can actually alter the effects of adversity by releasing a spirit of giving in every area of your life.

The second way to overcome adversity is to *do*. The Hebrew word for "do" is *"asah."* It is used over 1,000 times in the Old Testament. Genesis 7:5 says, *"And Noah did according unto all that the Lord commanded him."* As a Christian, you are to *do* what God has commanded. Defeated Christians walk around looking like they have been chewing on glass. They are miserable because they do not *do* God's will.

What has God commanded you to do? Preach the gospel, heal the sick, set the captives free, feed the hungry, and minister to those who are in prison—all in the name of Jesus. You have to be a *doer* of God's Word, not just a hearer.

Doing the will of God can empower you to face and overcome adversity. When you are up to your neck in trouble, it is easy to spend time on yourself, "I don't have time to think about God right now. Besides, when this passes, I will do whatever God wants me to do. But not right now." You tend to focus on yourself and make excuses. Unless you do God's bidding, you will never reverse the curse. Adversity will reign in your life, and you will be crippled by it.

Honor the Lord

The third way to overcome adversity is through worship. The Hebrew word for worship is *"chabah,"* meaning "to bow down and honor the Lord." Worship is actually a form of spiritual warfare. When you are hurting, the devil wants you to strike back, to try and get even. God wants you to submit to Him, and let Him turn what was meant for evil into a blessing for your life.

Remember, you are a citizen of God's kingdom. The east wind may blow—and it may blow hard—but it will not destroy you if your heart is set on worshipping the Lord. Do not sleep through hardship.

Wake up! Do not meditate on your problems. Rebuke the devil in the name of Jesus, and meditate on the promises of a loving, faithful God. Stay in the Word, and stop feeling sorry for yourself. Realize you are blessed in Jesus!

Get into a blessing mode. You will not be overcome by depression if you apply these principles. Neutralize the enemy as soon as you awaken in the morning, and then start to praise God for what He has done in your life. Remember His goodness, and develop a grateful heart.

Studies indicate that your mind believes what you say to yourself more than what other people say to you. When you curse yourself, your mind believes it. When you say, "I am so stupid; I'll never amount to anything," your mind accepts that as truth.

Rebuke the devil in the name of Jesus and renew your mind! Get into the Word, and begin to speak blessings. Then, do the works of the Lord. Do not concentrate on sickness. Meditate on the healing virtue of Jesus. Remember the people God has healed. Then, step out in faith and begin ministering to the sick. Do not think about your own condition; reverse the curse. Ask God to give you an anointing for healing. By praying for other people, you will disarm the devil.

Finally, worship the Lord in a spirit of humility. Repent of pride and adopt a teachable attitude. Develop a spirit of adoration and praise. Nurture gentleness in your heart.

Draw Closer to God

When I was seventeen years old, I enlisted in the armed forces. That January, I was sent to Korea. Let me tell you, it is COLD in Korea, especially in January. I was new to the service, and far away from home. To make things worse, I could not find anyone in the village who spoke English. It seemed the wind of adversity had ripped right through my heart and left me empty and alone.

As I considered my circumstances, I decided to go for a walk. Before long, I came to a mountain. I climbed to the top and began walking across it. Then, I heard yelling. I looked down and saw the village people waving their arms. They were yelling at me! I could not imagine why they would be so upset.

I stopped in my tracks, looked up to heaven, and said, "God, I need *You*." Then, in an unexplained moment of faith, I blessed Him for taking care of me. The loneliness left me, and somehow, I felt as though life was not quite as tough as it had seemed moments before.

I later discovered that the mountain had a Buddhist shrine on top of it, and, evidently, I was walking on Buddha's head. That is why they were yelling at me.

Three years later, a Korean pastor named Paul Yonggi Cho purchased the mountain and turned that place, with its Buddhist shrine, into a "house of prayer." Today, thousands if not millions of people come to Prayer Mountain to intercede on behalf of others in *the name of Jesus!*

It never dawned on me that God would use those days of loneliness and adversity to draw me to Him and to build up my faith, but that is exactly what He did.

Adversity *can* work in your favor! If you humble yourself and seek the Lord, adversity must work for you and not against you.

Let Conflict Be a Catalyst

Think about this for a moment: everything of significance that has ever happened in history has come through pressure. Enormous conflict not only led to the discovery of electricity, but it also led to the invention of the telephone and the airplane. Conflict causes men of faith to persevere in the face of defeat. Indeed, conflict can be an important catalyst for your spiritual breakthrough.

Although I was not an "A" student when I went to Bible school, I understood the value of perseverance. I had experienced so much hell in my life that I was driven to prayer. I lived on my knees and in the Word throughout my days in Bible school. Some people in my class thought I was the "most likely to fail," but I did not let failure reign in my life. I was desperate to hear from God, and as a result, God used that time to develop character in me.

If you want to overcome adversity, you *must* be willing to persevere. God does not always give us immediate answers, or immediate relief, but He is a faithful and loving Father—and He *does* answer us when the time is right.

Be Filled with the Holy Spirit

When I first learned about the Holy Spirit and about praying in tongues, I went to a hotel and prayed for three days and nights. I needed God's power to face the pressure that seemed to surround me. I prayed all night long.

A few days later, I was scheduled to speak at a church. As I sat in the pastor's office and waited for the service to start, God began to show me a vision. In it, I saw His Word, lying in a field. I heard a voice speak to the Word. It quoted Mark 11:24, *"Therefore I say unto you, What things soever ye desire, when ye pray, believe that ye receive them, and ye shall have them."* Then, the voice simply said, "Rise up."

The verse shook itself loose and stood right up. Then, the voice addressed another verse, then another, and another. Thousands of Scriptures stood up—all of them promises from the Father.

The wind began to blow. It blew in a circular direction, and the promises turned into mighty, warring angels.

I asked God what the vision meant, and He said, "Son, My Word is Spirit and Life. I have sent it as an army on your behalf. Believe it and walk in it."

That vision came when I was facing a time of great adversity. As

I spoke to the congregation that night, I sensed the presence and anointing of God, and I saw the Lord do many wonderful things. A doctor was healed. So were several other people. God touched hearts and lives and blessed many individuals.

The pressures I had to confront caused me to seek the Lord's face. It was not easy. In fact, there were times when I felt like giving up, but I did not. I persevered and the reward was great. I found deeper intimacy with the Lord, and fruitfulness in His kingdom.

Ask for God's Protection

I learned the importance of God's protection on one of my trips to the Middle East. The Lord had told me to go to Lebanon and preach to the marines. A man I knew offered to go along to pray and minister as God directed. I consented, since he considered himself to be a man of faith, and I want to be with faith-filled Christians, especially in volatile settings like that one.

When we got to Jerusalem, Israeli Intelligence warned us that the PLO was planning to bomb the area we intended to visit. The situation was serious, and they advised us to go only when they determined it was safe for us to travel.

By the time I reached my room and changed clothes, my friend was fast asleep. I woke him up, and he said point-blank to me, "I am not going."

"What do you mean? I thought you were a faith person," I said.

"Yes, but they are killing people out there. This isn't like going to church, you know," he replied.

I was not sure what to do, so I prayed all night long. At about 2:00 AM, the Spirit of God told me it was time to "wash some feet." I emptied the trashcan and filled it with water. Then, I put it in the middle of the room and told my friend to get out of bed, in Jesus' name. I said, "Put your feet in this trash can, brother."

Despite his reservations, he got up and did as I asked. Then, an amazing thing happened. He started to cry. The Spirit of God fell on him, and he said, "Okay, I'll go!"

The PLO bombed the area 15 minutes before we arrived in the city of Sidon. Had we gotten there any earlier, we would have been hit. But, God protected us. We headed out when *He* told us to go, not when Israeli Intelligence said we should. We reached Beirut safely and preached deliverance and hope to the marines stationed there.

I wish I could say the trip back to Jerusalem was easier, but it definitely wasn't. It was downright frightening. The Muslims told us we had to evacuate the area before 3:00 a.m. because there was going to be a battle. We started to drive across a bridge but had to turn back when we were caught in the crossfire. As we reversed our course, I said, "We'll have to go faster, brother; if the PLO can see us well enough to shine their spotlights in our faces, they'll shoot us."

We were driving as fast as we could through the streets of Lebanon. Somehow, we took a wrong turn and found ourselves headed directly into a PLO funeral procession. It did not help that we were in an Israeli vehicle with Israeli license plates! The situation could not have been any worse, or so I thought. The PLO was both in front of us and behind us.

I was really scared! I started thinking about the television specials I had hosted: "Let My People Go!" and "Israel, America's Key to Survival." I thought, "What if these guys recognize me?" I turned sharply—and realized it was, once again, a wrong turn!

We could take only one road and it led to Damascus and Syria. We drove over a mountain and headed straight into Damascus. Our situation was becoming more serious by the moment. I was a born-again Jew, on my way back to Israel after preaching to American marines stationed in hostile territory. *What if they caught me?*

Then, I looked at the gas gauge. We were almost out of gas. I stopped the car, took the lights off the license plate, and said, "It's time to pray." In those few moments of crisis, I called out to God, "Lord, in the name of Jesus, we need a miracle, and we need it NOW!"

While we were praying, an Arab walked up to the vehicle. He said, "May I help you?"

"Yes, we need some gas," I answered.

Miraculously, he gave us the gas we needed. Then, he got into the car and showed us exactly where to go! I tried to pay him for his help, but he only gave me a piece of change in return. God used an Arab to drive us through the blackness of night, through PLO territory, through a raging battle, back to safety!

When we got to the border, the Israeli guard asked, "How did you get back here? We made a terrible mistake; we were supposed to put you in a Lebanese cab, not an Israeli vehicle. I cannot believe you are all right! No one has ever traveled from Israel to Beirut and back in an Israeli civilian vehicle!"

God protected us and taught me a vital lesson about obedience and trust. By His grace, we were able to lead a Hispanic marine to the Lord during that trip. Three weeks later, he was killed in Beirut.

The Lord says you are to be strong in the midst of adversity. Do not buckle under pressure. Deal with it in the spiritual realm. Be filled with praise, and worship the Lord. Do not feel sorry for yourself. Do what God has called you to do!

When adversity strikes, you are more likely to become vulnerable spiritually, physically, mentally, and emotionally. Do not try to "go it alone." Let other Believers pray with you and stand against the enemy. Ask for and expect God's protection.

Stay humble in your spirit. Be sensitive to God so you can do His will. You will be stronger in your faith and closer to the heart of God as you face—and overcome—the wind of adversity.

CHAPTER THIRTEEN

Let Jesus Be Your Source

Acknowledge God as your Source, put your faith in
Him, and He will roll your stones away!

Some time ago, I prayed at the sepulcher of Jesus in Jerusalem. A sign that reads, "He is not here—He is risen" hangs on the door of the empty tomb. Mark 16:1-3 says, *"And when the sabbath was past, Mary Magdalene, and Mary the mother of James, and Salome, had bought sweet spices, that they might come and anoint him. And very early in the morning the first day of the week, they came unto the sepulcher at the rising of the sun. And they said among themselves. Who shall roll us away the stone from the door of the sepulcher?"*

Verse 4 says that the stone "was *very great.*" Who could roll away a stone, which weighed several thousand pounds? Yet, the next two verses tell us the stone was already moved when the two women arrived. "And entering into the sepulcher, they saw a young man sitting on the right side, clothed in a long white garment; and they were affrighted. And he saith unto them, Be not affrighted: Ye seek Jesus of Nazareth, which was crucified: he is risen; he is not here: behold the place where they laid him."

In verse 9, Jesus makes His first appearance. *"Now when Jesus was risen early the first day of the week, he appeared first to Mary Magdalene, out of whom he had cast seven devils."* Isn't it amazing that Jesus would appear *first* to Mary Magdalene, a former prostitute who had been transformed into a woman of great faith?

Imagine yourself in Jerusalem. It's Sunday morning, the first day of the week. Your Lord has been brutally killed and buried. Your dreams for the future have been shattered. Then you hear that the huge stone has been rolled away by the power of the Holy Spirit. Would you believe it? Is the truth of it a reality in your life today?

Like Jesus' followers, many Christians want to hang on to the stone. There are stones in your life that God wants to roll away—if only you will make Him your source.

The Problem with Stones

For 4,000 years, the Jewish people have had serious problems with stones. I made this statement to the Russian Jews who had converted to Christianity when I was preaching in Israel one time. When these Jewish Christians came into the country, the government stuck them in the most desolate places, but they came from everywhere to hear the Word of God.

I reminded them that God told Abraham to leave his country and go into the Promised Land. In Genesis 15:7, He said He would give Abraham the land. "You have left your country and gone into the Promised Land," I told them, "and God has promised to bless those who bless thee."

Isaac woke up one morning, ready to inherit the blessing of Abraham. Later, when he had received the promise, he went to check out all that was supposed to be his, but it did not look very promising. The enemy had put stones in the wells, and there was no water. Without water, everything dies. It becomes desolate. The Bible says, *"With joy shall you draw water out of the wells of salvation"* (Isaiah 12:3). Just as Isaac had to get the stones out of the wells to get to the water, you have to get the stones out of your life so they don't block the flow of Jesus in you.

Jesus Is Alive!

On resurrection morning, a living Christ rose from the dead to roll all the stones away, but those who did not acknowledge God as their Source were still in defeat.

Jesus was risen. He was Lord. He was alive! Mark 16:11-14 says that when Mary Magdalene told His disciples that Jesus was alive, they did not believe her. *"Afterward he appeared unto the eleven as they sat at meat, and upbraided them with their unbelief and hardness of heart, because they believed not them which had seen him after he was risen."*

Many people today do not believe that Jesus is alive, but I have more faith in His existence than I have in your existence. Why? Because I have seen Him.

When I was just 11 years old, Jesus appeared to me in my room. I saw the scars in His hands, and He told me what He was going to do with my life. He has fulfilled every word of that promise. He is risen. He is alive!

Everything within me said He could not be alive. My Jewish mother told me He was dead. My relatives and their religious traditions said He did not even exist. When He looked into my face and said, "Son, I love you and I have a great plan for your life," I knew He was alive.

When you make God your Source and put your faith completely in Him, He will roll the stones of life away. Do not be among the shallow Christians who spend all their time asking God to fix their problems but avoid any real intimacy with Him. They want relief but not true release.

Jesus came so you could experience God full blast, so He could kick the walls of your life down, bind defeat and discouragement, and bring you happiness. The choice is yours. You can continue to face your problems by yourself, or you can allow Jesus to be your Source.

The Keys to Hell and Death

How do you get the stones rolled out of your life? Believe that He is risen in *your* life. Arm yourself with His power and become dangerous to *every* demonic spirit you encounter.

Many people say, "I don't believe in being militant." Well, my Bible tells me about a mighty Lord who appeared to the apostle John on the Isle of Patmos. In Revelation 1:17-18, John said, *"And when I saw him, I fell at his feet as dead. And he laid his right hand upon me, saying unto me, 'Fear not; I am the first and the last: I am he that liveth, and was dead; and behold, I am alive for evermore, Amen; and have the keys of hell and of death."*

When you acknowledge God as your Source, you have the keys to hell and death. You do not fear death, man, the past, the present, or anything that the devil sends your way. You may be knocked down, but you will never be knocked out.

There are thousands of born-again, spirit-filled Russian Jews who live in Israel right now. They know God is their Source—He led them there for a purpose. Actually, the state of Israel brought them in, not realizing that God, in His prophetic plan, would use them to evangelize the nation.

When we ministered to them recently, it was the first meeting to be held in the nation since these Russian Jews had come together. I preached a message on the fire of God, because we were near Mt. Carmel where Elijah the prophet called fire down from heaven. I said to them, "God has made you flames of fire."

Suddenly, these Jews started having visions. One of them started to cry and said, "I see a flame of fire and angels." Many were being baptized in the Holy Spirit, even though we were not praying for that specifically. They have so many miracle testimonies.

Why are they seeing miracle after miracle? They believe in God as their Source; they know He can roll the stones away.

Once you realize that Jesus has conquered death and the grave, that He has the keys to hell, and you acknowledge Him as your Source, He puts faith in you and takes fear out of you. When faith operates in your life, the walls come down and the stones in your life are rolled away.

A Great and Mighty Work

Since I was on my way to Moscow, those Russian Jews gave me a letter to give to the Jews still living in the former Soviet countries.

It was a prophetic letter. They had posted it in their churches. It said, "Come home to the land of Israel. Come home according to the prophecies. The Lord is pouring out His Holy Spirit. Join us in this great end-time revival."

God is doing a great work on the earth. He is moving today in a mighty way. Right now while you are reading this, a huge printing press is running in Beijing, China. It is the press that former Chairman Mao Tse-tung used to print his infamous *Little Red Book*.

Years ago, the Chinese foreign minister signed a document, allowing the gospel of Jesus Christ to be printed. So far, over one million New Testaments have been produced and put on Siberian trains to Russia. Think of it! Bibles coming from the same presses that Chairman Mao once used to print communist materials of death and doom!

In addition, the Pentagon recently received a most unusual request. It was an official request from the high offices of the Soviet Union, asking for born-again evangelical chaplains for their military.

God is doing a mighty work indeed!

God Is Moving

God is moving in a big way, a way that will usher in the return of Jesus Christ. When you think of the ongoing turmoil in the Middle East, you may say, "I don't know why the Persian Gulf War had to happen." Do you realize that there were over 25,000 born-again Pentecostal Christians on Muslim soil in Saudi Arabia, Kuwait, and other Arab countries during that war? And yes, they were talking about Jesus.

There is a battle to be won, and God is not going to stop until all the stones are rolled away. He is in the stone-rolling business. All He needs is a stone—and faith—and He will do the rest.

He has spoiled principalities and powers before. Take heart! You can march big, shout big, and believe big! No matter what your problems are—whether financial, emotional, or people problems, or circumstances beyond your control—they will be resolved if you give them to Jesus. Once upon a time, there was a dismal Friday, but Sunday was just around the corner! There *will* be a resurrection!

I was in the room with Russian Jews, sharing a prophetic word, when God spoke to my heart: "This is the revival of which I have spoken. It has begun, and Satan will not stop it. Nor will he stop My return. This move will usher in My coming."

A reporter from *The Jerusalem Post* said, "We heard you speaking. You believe that Jerusalem is the capital of Israel. Why?" I opened my Bible and read the Scripture from Acts that says, *"Ye men of Galilee, why stand ye gazing up into heaven? This same Jesus, which is taken up from you into heaven, shall so come in like manner as ye have seen him go into heaven. Then returned they unto Jerusalem from the mount called Olivet, which is from Jerusalem a sabbath day's journey"* (Acts 1:11-12). I reminded him that the Mount of Olives is where Jesus ascended into Heaven—and I said, "He is coming back to the Mount of Olives."

Later, I read the article he had written. In it, I had proclaimed the Lordship of Jesus. I had said, "Tell it to the city of Jerusalem, tell it to the nation of Israel—Jesus will return."

The Messiah Is Coming

Right now, all over Israel there are huge banners that declare, "The Messiah is coming, the Messiah is coming." They know that, according to prophecy, the Messiah *is* coming.

When we left Jerusalem, we flew to Holland where Corrie ten Boom lived. We went into her home, which we have restored and made into a witness for the Lord. Hers is such an incredible story, and we knew it would touch the Jewish people.

While we were there for a meeting, it was Liberation Week in Holland. The country decided to spotlight the ten Boom clock shop and home as a symbol of liberation.

Holland is a country that does not permit the gospel to be proclaimed on its television stations, yet they gave us two hours of prime time. The whole nation saw the movie, *"The Hiding Place."* The station then gave us time at the end of the broadcast to talk about Corrie ten Boom and the Jesus she knew. We were also on three national radio stations! Stones will be rolled away if you let God be your Source!

Later, an 81-year-old woman came up to Carolyn and me and said, "I was twenty-three years old when they took me from my home and put me in a concentration camp. I did not know anything about Jesus or God except that I hated them. There were two girls on the bunk above me. One was Corrie, and the other was her sister, Betsie."

"Betsie was very ill. When the guards gave bread to them, Corrie and Betsie gave part of it to others and had communion. I listened to them singing songs. I turned to them and asked, 'How can you believe in God and Jesus when we are all going to die? How can you sing in this hellish place?'"

"Corrie looked at me and said, "Because Jesus is alive.'"

That elderly woman gave her heart to Jesus Christ because of two women who refused to be defeated by the darkness of hell, but believed instead that Jesus is alive. She said, "I am alive today because of Corrie and Betsie ten Boom."

Ye Shall Receive Power

What happens when the stones are rolled away in your life? Acts 1:8 says, *"But ye shall receive power, after that the Holy Ghost is come upon you: and ye shall be witnesses unto me."* You may say, "I know all about Jesus." But that means nothing. Jesus hung on a cross, taking upon His own body *your* sins, so that you might have peace with God.

John 3:16-18 says, *"For God so loved the world that He gave His only begotten Son, that whosoever believeth in Him should not perish, but have everlasting life. For God sent not His son into the world to condemn the world; but that the world through him might be saved. He that believeth on him is not condemned."* Revelation 3:20 says, *"Behold, I stand at the door, and knock: if any man* (or woman) *hear my voice, and open the door, I will come in to him, and will sup with him and he with me."*

Your perspective of yourself will determine the possibilities you pursue. When God is your Source, you won't have a bad self-image.

No matter what the devil has done to you in the past, when you have resurrection life, the keys to hell and death, the power of the Holy Spirit, the Living Word in your being, you won't ever see yourself as defeated.

You will pursue greatness because you serve a great God. Just as He turned Mary Magdalene into a woman of great faith, God turns captives into conquerors when the stones of life are rolled away.

CHAPTER FOURTEEN
Let Faith Prevail

You can have prevailing faith. Just acknowledge God
as your Source, and believe His Word.

D o you sometimes feel that your needs exceed your supply? Do you run out of money before you run out of bills? Do you feel physically drained? Are you afraid of emotional bankruptcy? Do you feel like you are spiritually starving? Again, whatever your need, God is your Source, and His provision is perfect!

First Kings 17 shows how God brought a drought to the land of Israel to punish Ahab, the King of Israel, for his wickedness. The drought lasted for 3 ½ years, and it resulted in a great famine. Yet, despite the shortage of food and water, God took care of Elijah. He told the prophet, *"And it shall be, that thou shalt drink of the brook; and I have commanded the ravens to feed thee there"* (1 Kings 17:4).

God used birds to feed Elijah, and He supplied water from a small stream. If you are facing a famine in your life, take heart! God has not forgotten you! He will meet your needs, even if He has to use birds and brooks!

Famine in the Land

The famine that hit Israel lasted a long time and was devastating. You may feel devastated by your circumstances today. You may have a serious shortage in your finances. You may feel pressured, worried, and upset. You may have unmet emotional needs, and as a result, you feel depressed and alone. You may be experiencing a physical setback through sickness, disease, mishap, or outright catastrophe. You can live in fear—or, you can turn your attention to the Source.

When you have calamity in your life, you can do one of two things: You can turn to God and learn from the experience, or you can give in to fear, worry, and unbelief.

If you permit fear and doubt to dominate your thinking in times of need, you will be unable to receive the provision God has for you. The dry period will escalate into a full-blown famine. You must be on guard during the dry times, or you will be overwhelmed by your own needs. When famine comes, you cannot talk yourself into abundance, or bargain your way out of debt. Famine will drain you of your life, energy, hope, joy, finances, and health.

Elijah's attitude was to focus on God's goodness and mercy, making the best of his situation and learning from this experience. He refused to let fear and unbelief dominate his thoughts. Instead, he was *grateful* to God. When there is a famine in the land, the Holy Ghost can assist you to demonstrate an attitude filled with gratitude, peace, and joy.

Elijah trusted God to meet all his needs and as a result, goodness, mercy, signs, wonders, and miracles followed. Elijah had faith that prevails. What about you? You can lose—or you can win. You can prevail—or you can fail. The choice is yours.

The Ravens Will Feed You

As Elijah came to the brook, the Lord said, *"I have commanded the ravens to feed thee there."* Isn't it comforting to know that God can supply your needs? He is not affected by your circumstances. He is not limited by your problems. He does not have to use conventional methods to care for you. He can feed you with the help of ravens!

The Jews considered ravens to be unclean. They were dumb scavengers, fearful of men, yet God chose to feed Elijah with these very birds. Had Elijah been religious, he would have rejected the food from the ravens based upon the Law. Instead, he could discern the word of the Lord and know it was His will. This method seems to be a contradiction. But God uses methods we never think of. Ravens were scavengers and were selected because they are more daring to approach a crowd of people to steal food, than any other bird.

Incidentally, the king was probably the only one with meat, and had his butchers prepared meals for the king, the ravens would fly down and grab the meat. But what is even more amazing is that the ravens had to be controlled by the Spirit of God. For them to give away their bounty was against their nature. Elijah was being fed from the king's table and his Source was God, not the ravens. If God did not manipulate nature, the ravens would never have turned themselves over to the prophet.

God will supply all your needs if you let Him—but He may not do it in a way you expect. He might surprise you. He might tell the ravens to feed you! That is all right. *Receive* His provision. Let the Holy Ghost lead you. Allow Him to meet your needs in the way He deems best. If you do not, you might just reject your Source.

Dry Brooks

It seems that Elijah was well cared for. The ravens brought him fresh bread and meat every morning and every night. He had cold, clean water to drink. He had everything he needed—until-the brook dried up. Rain had not fallen, and so the water eventually evaporated. As Elijah sat by the brook, he must have wondered why God had permitted his only source of water to vanish. Do you ever feel like that? Do you wonder why you are so spiritually dry, emotionally void, close to financial ruin, or weary and desolate? Sometimes, God allows you to go through dry periods so you will thirst for *Him*. Hosea 10:12 says, *"Sow to yourselves in righteousness, reap in mercy; break up your fallow ground; for it is time to seek the Lord, till he come and rain righteousness upon you."*

Your "brook" may be as dry as a bone, but that does not mean God has abandoned you. He is ready to meet your needs! He is happy to meet them! But you must seek *Him*.

As soon as the brook dried up, God told Elijah what to do next. In verse 9, He says, *"Arise, get thee to Zarephath, which belongeth to Zidon, and dwell there: behold, I have commanded a widow woman there to sustain thee."*

In the natural, that sounds crazy. "Now, son, I want you to go to the next town and knock on a stranger's door. Tell her you want to live in her house for a while. It will be all right. Trust Me." What would you do? Would you obey God, or would you let fear and embarrassment keep you from having your needs met?

Elijah chose to obey God. He did not care what anyone thought or said. He trusted the Lord, and God not only met his needs, He also used Elijah to save the life of the widow and her son.

Verses 12-15 says, *"And she said, As the Lord thy God liveth, I have not a cake, but an handful of meal in a barrel, and a little oil in a cruse: and, behold, I am gathering two sticks, that I may go in and dress it for me and my son, that we may eat it, and die. And Elijah said unto her, Fear not; go and do as thou hast said: but make me thereof a little cake first, and bring it unto me, and after make for thee and for thy son. For thus saith the Lord God of Israel, The barrel of meal shall not waste, neither shall the cruse of oil fail, until the day that the Lord sendeth rain upon the earth. And she went and did according to the saying of Elijah: and she, and he, and her house, did eat many days. "*

The Widow's Miracle

Why did God allow the brook to dry up? I believe there were two reasons: First, He was giving Elijah an opportunity to obey His voice, and second, He knew the widow needed a miracle.

Elijah's willingness to do what the Lord asked allowed the Lord to demonstrate His provision for the prophet and for the widow and her son. When God tells you to do something, remember this story. He may want to use the occasion to meet not only your needs but the needs of someone else as well.

Elijah stayed at the widow's house for some time, and God took care of the three of them. They had enough meal and oil to last through the famine. It was a great testimony to the people of her town, I'm sure.

Then, just when life was bearable again, tragedy struck. Verse 17 says, *"And it came to pass after these things, that the son of the woman, the mistress of the house, fell sick; and his sickness was so sore, that there was no breath left in him."* Imagine what she must have thought. "Here I have opened my house to a man of God. I have seen a miracle performed through the meal and oil. But now, my only son has died."

In verse 18, she said to Elijah, *"...What have I to do with thee, O thou man of God? art thou come unto me to call my sin to remembrance, and to slay my son?"* How do you respond when tragedy strikes? Do you blame yourself? Do you blame God? Do you turn against God's people?

Verses 19-21 gives the prophet's answer, *"And he said unto her, Give me thy son. And he took him out of her bosom, and carried him up into a loft, where he abode, and laid him upon his own bed. And he cried unto the Lord, and said, O Lord my God, hast thou also brought evil upon the widow with whom I sojourn, by slaying her son? And he stretched himself upon the child three times, and cried unto the Lord, and said, O Lord my God, I pray thee, let this child's soul come into him again."*

This was a terrible moment for Elijah. He had heard the voice of God and obeyed Him repeatedly, and despite his obedience, the widow's son fell sick and died. Life is not always easy for the people of God. Sometimes there are terrible moments when there is nothing you can do but cry out in desperation to God.

Several years ago, my oldest daughter gave birth to triplets and there were complications. They were born prematurely and we could have given in to fear. The situation was certainly serious enough. Instead, we cried out to the Lord. For several weeks, we prayed and sought God's face. We asked for mercy and healing, and God answered. He strengthened the babies so that they were able to go home.

God also heard Elijah's prayer and healed the widow's son. Verses 23 says, *"And Elijah took the child, and brought him down out of the chamber into the house, and delivered him unto his mother: and Elijah said, See, thy son liveth."* And the woman said to Elijah, *"Now by this I know that thou art a man of God, and that the word of the Lord in thy mouth is truth."*

God brought a dead child back to life, but more importantly, He brought new life to the widow's dead spirit. Prior to this experience, she had respect for God, but she did not know Him as her Lord. When she saw life return to the body of her little boy, something deep within her heart was stirred. For the first time, she *knew* the Word of God was true and worthy of her trust.

God is a God who gives and gives and gives and gives. He is a good God, and His generosity is the basis for the biblical principle of sowing and reaping.

Have you ever told someone, "You're going to reap what you sow"? That statement is true. If you plant tomato seeds, you will harvest tomatoes. If you sow love, you will reap love. If you sow mercy, you will reap mercy. If you sow into the kingdom of God with your finances, He will bless you. Galatians 6:7-8 says, *"Be not deceived; God is not mocked: for whatsoever a man soweth, that shall he also reap. For he that soweth to his flesh shall of the flesh reap corruption; but he that soweth to the Spirit shall of the Spirit reap life everlasting."*

In the beginning, the widow had to give Elijah the last bit of meal and oil she had; she had to sow her meager supplies in order to reap abundant provision from the Lord. In other words, she had to exercise her faith. Later, she had to turn her dead son over to the hands of a prophet in order to receive him back alive. She could have sown to her flesh, but she did not; she chose to exercise her faith.

Had the widow refused to obey God, either by denying Elijah the last of her meal and oil or by refusing to give him her dead son, the result would have been death. By turning to God, she found life for herself and for her son—and faith that prevails.

Is God asking you to exercise your faith today? In what impossible situations is He asking you to demonstrate your trust? Are you sowing what you want to reap? Or, are you planting seeds of fear and doubt?

You *will* reap what you sow. If you are in need today, turn to the Lord. Trust Him to provide; then obey His voice. Exercise your faith in the name of Jesus. Give Him room to move in your life as He wills.

Then, plant seeds of mercy, patience, kindness, love, joy, and peace, and watch the Holy Ghost produce a rich harvest in your life— and in the lives of those around you.

The Prayer of Faith

Acts 12:1-17 tells the story of Peter's arrest. Herod set about persecuting the church, and in the process killed James, the brother of

John. Verse 3 says, *"And because he saw it pleased the Jews, he proceeded further to take Peter also...."* He threw Peter in jail.

It was a dark time for God's people. Brutal Roman soldiers were hunting them, and one by one, their leaders were either killed or imprisoned. To their credit, the disciples asked the Lord to help Peter. Verse 5 says, *"...prayer was made without ceasing of the church unto God for him."*

They prayed all night. The only problem was that they were filled with unbelief. God miraculously released Peter, and when he knocked at the gate of the house where they were meeting, the disciples did not believe he was really there!

Verses 13-16 say, *"And as Peter knocked at the door of the gate, a damsel came to hearken, named Rhoda. And when she knew Peter's voice, she opened not the gate for gladness, but ran in, and told how Peter stood before the gate. And they said unto her, Thou art mad. But she constantly affirmed that it was even so. Then said they, It is his angel. But Peter continued knocking: and when they had opened the door, and saw him, they were astonished."*

Rhoda was so excited to hear Peter's voice; she did not stop to let him in. She just ran back and told the others. "Hey, guess what! Peter's here! That's right; he's just outside the gate!" They didn't believe her.

"You're crazy," they said. "Peter's in jail. It must be his angel." It was only by the grace of God, and by Rhoda's persistence, that Peter was allowed to enter the house of his friends! When you pray, be ready to receive God's answer! Expect a miracle. Trust His Word, and allow Him to be God.

James 5:16 says, *"Confess your faults one to another, and pray one for another, that ye may be healed. The effective fervent prayer of a righteous man availeth much."*

Do not try to dictate how God should answer your prayers, or when. He knows what you need, and He knows the best way to meet your needs. Remember, He is a good God!

Mary, the mother of Jesus, said in Luke 1:38, *"...be it unto me according to thy word..."* That is one of the most powerful statements a person could make. You will never accomplish all that God has for you unless you submit yourself to the Word of God. You can have prevailing faith; just acknowledge God as your Source, and believe His Word.

When Needs Arise, Release Faith

Signs, wonders, goodness, and mercy are all following you in your time of need. Miracles rarely occur during times of plenty; they occur when you have needs and dare to release your faith. Are you releasing your faith today? Or, are you releasing a string of emotions? The needs in your life will either prompt you to respond or react—you will either respond in faith to God, or react in frustration, fear, and anger for your circumstances.

Prevailing faith does not make rash judgments in times of need. Prevailing faith does not let anger dictate actions. It does not make demands. Prevailing faith rests in peace and joy, and allows God to move as He sees fit. Prevailing faith says, "God, You are my Source, Your Word is true, and I believe it. It is settled, and I am going forward in the name of Jesus."

A Word from God

I was speaking at First Assembly in Little Rock, Arkansas, one day when I received a call about a young man named Randy Van Pay. My wife Carolyn called to tell me he had been injured in an automobile accident.

He was pulling out onto the road when a speeding car rammed into his. Randy's car was smashed, and he was thrown out.

His heart stopped three times before the EMTs got him to the hospital. His entire left side was crushed. One lung collapsed, and the other was barely functioning.

His parents called my wife and told her it looked like he was not going to make it. Carolyn immediately began to pray and as she did, God gave her a promise: "I will heal him and bring glory to the mourners."

I joined my wife and together, we fought for Randy in prayer. I refused to get angry at the other driver, or judge Randy, or get angry with God. I was awakened one morning at 2:00, and I felt as if the devil were choking me.

The devil said, "I am going to kill Randy. His parents won't be saved. He will die tonight." Frankly, I could not see through the eyes of faith at that moment. My eyes were seeing Randy and the grip death had on him, but finally, through the work of the Holy Ghost, I began to see in the Spirit.

I said to the devil, "Kill him. Be my guest, but in the morning God will raise him from the dead." I could not have said that if Carolyn and I had not heard from God. I would not presume on the Holy Ghost. But we had a definite word from God, and I knew He would perform what He had promised.

I See Randy Healed

That morning, Carolyn and I drove from Little Rock, to Orange, Texas, praying in the Holy Spirit all the way. When we arrived, it was late, so we went straight to bed.

The next morning, I drove to the hospital. As I drove I kept repeating, "God, I thank you that Randy is healed. I see Randy healed. I believe that Randy is healed."

I walked into his room in the intensive care unit and saw him lying on the bed, with tubes running everywhere. Fluid was draining out of his lungs. He had several monitors attached.

"Randy Van Pay," I said

He put his hand over his tracheotomy and said, "Yes?"

"You look wonderful. You are healed. Your head is healed. Your chest and lungs are healed. God has sent me here to tell you that you are totally healed, Randy."

"I am healed," Randy replied. He reached up and pulled the tubes out, and immediately, the machines went crazy. The hospital staff ran us out of his room. I am sure they thought we were dangerous fanatics.

Fifteen minutes later, a nurse came downstairs with big tears running down her face. She said, "I don't understand what happened. I just do not understand. Your friend is sitting in a chair outside the door of the ICU. His lungs are perfect. There is no fluid anywhere. His heart is working perfectly. There does not seem to be anything wrong with him. He is just sitting there, resting in a chair!"

I said, "There *is* nothing wrong. He has been healed."

Past the Drought to the River

You may be experiencing a dry time in your life right now. You may have cried out to God and asked why He abandoned you. You may have complained about His lack of provision. You may have let fear and anger rule your heart and determine your course of action.

You may have faced tragedy, the death of a child, a divorce, financial failure, a crisis in your health. You may have despaired, even as the widow in First Kings 17 despaired.

But look up! God is still on the throne. He has not turned His back on you, not for one moment! He knows you are hurting, and He understands your anger and frustration, but He wants you to be healed in the name of Jesus.

Look in the Spirit and see past the drought and famine, past your difficulties. See a river of life, a pool, a stream, a brook, a raven, a resurrection. See and receive faith that prevails.

CHAPTER FIFTEEN

Have a Breakthrough, Not a Breakdown

*The more you allow the Holy Spirit to be Himself in
you, the more you are strengthened.*

I hear the term "spiritual burnout" a lot. But frankly, there is no
such thing as spiritual burnout. Burnout is either emotional or
mental, and both happen when a person is double minded, when
he is wavering between a life of righteousness in Christ Jesus and a
life of carnality.

The Holy Spirit does not burn out—the human spirit does. The
more you allow the Holy Spirit to be Himself in you, the more you
are strengthened.

Acts 1:8 says, *"You shall receive power after the Holy Ghost has
come upon you to be my witnesses both in Jerusalem, Judea, Samaria,
and unto the uttermost parts of the earth."*

Many Christians, especially Pentecostals, think the only function
of the Holy Spirit is to enable them to speak in tongues. Remember,
even demons can speak in tongues—not the tongues of angels, but
those that falsify the Holy Spirit.

Some people even go so far as to say, "speaking in tongues is the initial evidence" of having received the Holy Spirit. I would like to tell you something. There are a few other evidences, such as a life that has been transformed! God gave you "power" so you can be His witness.

The early Church had a powerful hunger for a spiritual breakthrough. Believers knew nothing could be accomplished without it.

Sadly, there are people today who do not understand this important difference. Some Christians think that getting saved and getting baptized in the Holy Spirit ten years ago is all you need. Well, it is not all you need!

Step Out in Faith

Four steps will help you have a breakthrough, and avoid a breakdown. The Bible says you are to walk in the footsteps of Jesus.

SETTLE in your mind that Jesus reigns as King.

TRUST God's Word completely.

ENCOURAGE yourself in the Lord.

PUT Jesus first.

Revelation 11:15 says, *"The kingdoms of this world are become the kingdoms of our Lord, and of his Christ; and he shall reign for ever and ever."*

So many Christians spend their lives trying to make Jesus King. You can't make Him King—He is already King. You cannot crown Him King—He has already been crowned. You cannot make Him Lord—He is already Lord.

You can *acknowledge* His Kingship and His Lordship and then walk in it. You cannot make Him King or Lord. That is what religious people try to do. They also try to get God to help them defeat the devil. God will not help you defeat the devil because He has already defeated him. Settle in your mind that Jesus reigns as King.

Replace Stinking Thinking

The Bible says Jesus Christ has already defeated all our enemies. He even took the sting out of death. You may say, "If Jesus has defeated the devil, eternally wounded and bruised him, and if Jesus is Lord and King, why don't I have a breakthrough?"

You could be a victim of what I call "stinking thinking"! This has to do with the way you see Jesus and the way you see yourself.

When you realize where Jesus is, your perspective is changed; you think differently about yourself and your circumstances. Where is Jesus right now? He is sitting at the right hand of the Father. He is not in combat with the devil. He already won the victory at Calvary. He defeated the devil and destroyed his power, once and for all.

You need to realize what Jesus has done, that His name is above every name and He is the Living Word of God. When you see the truth and settle it in your heart, when you realize He is the reigning King, it will move you from the dimension of breakdown into breakthrough.

Christians who break down are people who have not settled things in their minds. If King Jesus is really reigning, you will not have a panic attack. *Acknowledge that God is your Source!* You will have a breakthrough when you accept His love and sovereignty.

Value God's Word

Second, trust God's Word. Look at what David said when he was discouraged, in the city of despair, beat up, and stressed out.

Psalm 3:6 says, *"I will not be afraid of ten thousands of people, that have set themselves against me round about."*

Psalm 27:3 says, *"Though a host should encamp against me, my heart shall not fear; though war should rise against me, in this will I be confident."*

Psalm 55:18 says, *"He hath delivered my soul in peace from the battle that was against me; for there were many with me."*

Over 200 times, the Old Testament describes God as the Lord of hosts. David used this term more than anyone, and with good reason. David said, "The Lord of hosts is with me." The Word of God is true—trust it more than anything else.

Believe that the Lord is closer than you think. Believe that the Lord is more committed than you think. Believe that God is more ambitious than you think. Believe in God's mighty words.

At times, you may have problems with words. You may get into disputing other people's words. Did you ever hear anyone call someone else a liar? It is easy not to have a lot of confidence in people's words.

However, your mistrust of others will desensitize you to the words of God, so when you hear His words you don't trust them as you should. Before you go to sleep at night, let the last words that go into your spirit be the words of God.

"The Lord of hosts is with me," David said.

In Hebrew, the word *"host"* means *"an army ready and poised for battle."* David also said, *"I am kept. The Lord keeps me."* The word *"kept"* in Hebrew means *"to hedge about as with thorns, to guard, to protect, to attend to."*

What is God saying to you today? Can you hear Him? Listen, He is saying, "Will you allow Me to be the Lord of hosts in your life?"

Focus on God

Most Christians do not have a philosophy by which they live—no objectives or goals. One positive thing I can say about my life is that I am focused. When God tells me to do something, nothing in this world can persuade me not to do it.

Why is that important? Because many people miss the blessings of God by allowing themselves to be distracted. They stop focusing on God and turn their attention to something else.

Many Christians panic when they find out they are sick, or when they are faced with financial troubles. Many Believers fall to pieces when things begin to go badly at home. Why? The reason is not that they do not believe Jesus heals the sick, or that He provides for our needs, or that He is the head of the home. They panic because they do not *focus* on the sovereignty of God, the greatness of the Lord of hosts, His grace, mercy, love and power.

As important as it is to memorize Bible verses, it is absolutely *essential* to focus your attention *on the Lord*. Studying the Scriptures, and knowing what they say about healing, for instance, will encourage you and raise the level of your faith in times of sickness, but your faith must be focused on the Lord. First, in order to believe you must confess and stand on the Scriptures that are relevant to your current situation, but your attention must be on God Himself. What is a healing scripture anyway? It is a word from Jesus, Who is your Healer.

Go to Jesus first! Settle in your mind who Jesus is and that He loves you. Then trust His Word completely. When you focus on Jesus, you will not cut yourself short with pride. He is the Lord of hosts. The battle is His—not yours.

Encourage Yourself

Third, encourage yourself in the Lord. In 1 Samuel 30:6, we read that although David was greatly distressed, he encouraged himself in the Lord.

Let me ask you this: Who says we must depend upon each other for encouragement? The world around us is totally co-dependent; it knows nothing of God's Word and His ability to encourage and strengthen us.

There is a dynamic truth in the Lord Jesus Christ and in His word that you learn when you are discouraged. Let me give you an example:

When you die, I can't do anything about it. No one can carry you through the valley of the shadow of death, except Jesus.

This is a private matter between you and Him. You can reach out to people for support, but there is a great difference in having a support system and being co-dependent.

Encourage yourself in the Lord. Ephesians 3:16 says, *"That he would grant YOU according to the riches of his glory to be strengthened with might by his Spirit in the inner man."*

Verse 20 says, *"Now unto him that is able to do exceedingly abundantly above all that we ask or think according to the power that worketh in us."*

One of the main reasons some Christians live in continual defeat is because they are ignorant regarding the sovereignty of Christ. They have not developed an intimacy with the Lord Jesus Christ. They do not walk and talk with Him.

Colossians 2:15 says, *"And having spoiled principalities and powers, he made a show of them openly, triumphing over them in it."*

Psalm 100:1-2 says, *"Make a joyful noise unto the Lord all ye lands. Serve the Lord with gladness. "*

Psalm 63:7 says, *"Because thou hast been my help, therefore in the shadow of thy wings will I rejoice."*

Nehemiah 8:10 says, *". . . for the joy of the Lord is your strength."*

Second Corinthians 3:17 says, *". . . where the Spirit of the Lord is there is liberty."*

How can you encourage yourself in the Lord? The only way is to spend time with Him. *You cannot be encouraged in the Lord if you are not nurturing your relationship with Him.* If you want to be filled with the Holy Spirit, get with Jesus!

Acknowledge God as Your Source

You can encourage yourself when you are walking with the Lord.

If you are going to walk in the kingdom of God on a daily basis, you cannot make the Church or any individual your source.

You cannot make your wife or your husband your source. No one can be your source but the Lord. If you make the Lord your Source, you will have a breakthrough—not a breakdown.

Encourage yourself. Get alone and start quoting the Scriptures and saying the same thing about yourself that God says about you. Get the joy of the Lord inside of you. The fruits of the Spirit are love, joy, peace, patience, kindness, goodness, faithfulness, gentleness, and self-control; they are not rejection, a bitter attitude, or a desire to play childish games with people.

Love will begin to come out of you, unconditional love. There will be peace, a contentment that comes when you are settled, a sense of calm, a quietness or stillness in your spirit—and there will be strength. Why? Because you have encouraged yourself in the Lord. You have built yourself up by your relationship with Jesus.

Put Jesus First

The last step is to put Jesus first. A song says, "Faith in God will move a mighty mountain."

One time we had two men visiting in our home. They had been cruelly tortured weekly in a concentration camp for seven years. They were given one bowl of soup a week, and on the tenth week, they would give it back to the Lord as a tithe.

Their captors put drugs in the soup to try to make them forget the scripture they knew. The guards tried to get the two to sign a confession that Jesus did not exist. This was part of an attempt to break the church of Romania.

The tormentors told one of the men that they were doing terrible things to his children and his wife because he would not sign their confession. I asked Richard, "How did you survive?"

He answered, "My physical body was breaking down, and I got all kinds of diseases. But I decided I was not going to worry about my physical body; rather, I was giving it to Jesus. Then my emotions were breaking down because of the drugs, so I just gave my mind to Jesus," he said.

He took every aspect of his life and laid it on an altar to God—at that point, his jailers could not hurt him anymore. He entered into a peace because he made Jesus Lord over his entire being.

One day the communists took him out in his weakened condition and told him they had complete power over him. They said if they hit him once he would fall and if they hit him twice he would die. He replied, "You have small power—I have big power."

"Do you still believe the Bible?" they asked.

"Yes," he answered.

Then they said, "The Bible says you are created in the image of God," and they held up a mirror in front of him. Richard saw the ugliest human being he had ever seen in his life. He was scarred from all the beatings he had received, and many of his bones were broken.

They said, "Your God must be ugly."

"Yes, on the cross He was so ugly no one would look upon Him. But after Calvary He became the most beautiful of them all. If you don't repent of your sins, you will be separated from this beautiful Jesus," Richard answered.

The communist guard picked up his club to hit Richard, and Richard said, "The first time you hit me I will say I love you. The second time you hit me—before I die—I will say I forgive you." The man started to cry, and he accepted Jesus Christ and was gloriously born again.

Why not put God first in every area of your life, right now, and have a breakthrough, not a breakdown?

CHAPTER SIXTEEN

Break the Spirit of Poverty

*If you want to break the spirit of poverty in your
mind, in your emotions, or in your finances, see God
as your Source.*

There are many types of poverty—spiritual, financial and emotional, just to name a few. When your dreams and visions do not happen as expected, poverty has an open door to your life—unless you know God as your Source. The spirit of poverty works hand in hand with the spirit of fear causing circumstances to seem impossible to overcome.

Bills continue to mount up and financial aid fails to come. You feel frustrated and angry. Depression sets in. You feel tired, alone, and overwhelmed. Worse, you begin to believe you are defeated. Kings 6:8 says, *"Then the king of Syria warred against Israel, and took counsel with his servants, saying, In such and such a place shall be my camp."*

That is just like the devil to say, "I am going to camp in your territory—in your house, with your husband, with your children, in the midst of your finances. I will camp at your weakest area." The Bible says the demons tremble at the name of Jesus. Satan becomes frightened when God is released in you, when you do not allow him to set up camp in your life. When you pinpoint what the devil is doing and are willing to deal with him on a *spiritual* level, you give him a panic attack.

As you stand against the wiles of the devil, God releases what you need. You begin to understand that He really is your Source, and that He is *faithful* to meet your needs.

God never runs short. He has ample resources for every spiritual problem you encounter. What's more, He *wants* to meet your need! He *wants* to release blessing into your life! He *wants* to release revelation knowledge. He *wants* to release wisdom. He *wants* to release the secret things you need to know—and break the spirit of poverty!

What Shall We Do?

In Second Kings 6, the king of Syria was looking for Elisha. When he found the prophet, the king surrounded the city with a great army. It was an intimidating sight, to say the least. Verse 15 says, *"And when the servant of the man of God was risen early, and gone forth, behold, an host compassed the city both with horses and chariots. And his servant said unto him, Alas, my master! How shall we do?"*

"What are we going to do?" the servant asked. "Five hundred thousand Syrians are circling the city, and no one is here to help us." That was the flesh talking—not the Spirit.

Have you ever wondered what you should do with a seemingly insurmountable problem? In verses 16-18 it says, *"Fear not: for they that be with us are more than they that be with them."* There were only two of them against 500,000 Syrians! What did Elisha see that his servant missed? *"And Elisha prayed, and said, 'Lord, I pray thee, open his eyes, that he may see.' And the Lord opened the eyes of the young man; and he saw: and behold, the mountain was full of horses and chariots of fire round about Elisha. And when they came down to him, Elisha prayed unto the Lord, and said, Smite this people, I pray thee, with blindness. And he smote them with blindness according to the word of Elisha."*

Elisha refused to let fear determine his response. He saw with Kingdom eyes and trusted God to save him. By faith, he defied the demons of hell. By faith, he led the blinded Syrian army right into the hands of the king of Israel!

By resisting the devil and submitting to God, Elisha was able to say to every demon spirit, principality, and power that was harassing him, "My servant and I are in agreement before the Lord; you are powerless here. And now, we will march you and your pagan army before the king of Israel."

The Spirit of Poverty

What is a spirit of poverty? A spiritual force drains you of everything you need in life. It robs you so that you do not have enough for God or for yourself. It steals from your family. It interferes with your work. It strips away your joy and confidence. It destroys your faith.

Sometimes a spirit of poverty blinds you so you cannot see what you need. It prevents you from knowing how to receive God's anointing to get the job done. At other times, you *know* what you need— but you never seem to have quite enough.

When you have a spirit of poverty, you must allow God to break its grip on your life. Do you need finances, joy, peace, strength, or anointing today? Does it seem that there is never enough to meet your needs? If so, you have a spirit of poverty on you. I'll say it again: the spirit of poverty *must* be broken before you can do the work of God.

A Borrowed Ax

The first few verses of Second Kings 6 tell us that one of the prophets was cutting down a tree with a borrowed ax when the iron ax head fell into the water. He was very upset, and asked Elisha what he should do.

In those days, iron was extremely precious, even more valuable than gold or silver, because it was the primary substance from which weapons of war were made. The Philistines had invented iron, and they used it to make great chariots that intimidated their enemies.

The prophet had borrowed someone's ax, and suddenly it was lost. Have you ever had anything like that happen to you? Have you ever lost something that was valuable, like a friendship or a marriage?

When a relationship is taken away, it is not uncommon to have mixed feelings about it; regret at having lost the relationship, fear of the unknown, guilt over your wrongdoing, anger that you were powerless to prevent the break. Despite the confusion, there remains a sense of indebtedness simply because that person meant something to you.

A spirit of poverty *feeds* off fear, guilt, anger, and confusion, and in the end, it produces debt in your life. That debt then produces pain, which is followed by a curse. To break free from the spirit of poverty, you must recognize it for what it is: a *spiritual problem*. The spirit of fear will try to grab you, but do not be fooled. Fear is not merely an emotion; the Bible says fear is "a spirit," and it does not come from God!

But faith is a spirit, also—and it *does* come from God. Every problem you have is a spirit-based problem that requires a Spirit-led solution.

Elisha said, "Let's go back and find the root of this problem. Let's look for the ax head." So, Elisha went and got himself a stick. He may have felt fearful since, in the natural, he had no way of retrieving the ax head from the water. After all, iron does not usually float. Nevertheless, Elisha did not let fear paralyze him. He knew the ax head was lost—unless God performed a miracle on his behalf. In his moment of need, Elisha dared to expect the impossible. He trusted the Lord because he *knew* God was his Source. He also recognized his problem as spiritual at its root.

Keep on Ticking

Some Christians think they are immune to problems and spiritual attacks just because they *are* Christians. But nothing could be further from the truth! The devil is hard at work, trying to undermine and defeat the people of God.

Acknowledging God as your Source does not mean you will not have needs. It does not mean you will not have battles to fight. However, it does mean that God will supply all your needs according to His riches in glory in Christ Jesus. It also means you will not have to fight the battles alone. The Lord will give you the strength to fight. In other words, you may take a licking, but you will keep on ticking!

The late singer-songwriter Mark Heard once said, "In the eye of the storm, the friends of God suffer no permanent harm."

When you know God as your Source, you do not let fear and adversity keep you from doing the right thing. You will not quit on people, you will not give up on your marriage, and you will not abandon your friendships, or turn your back on the family of God. You cannot—when you know God as your Source.

Believe the Word

Proverbs 18:21 says, *"Death and life are in the power of the tongue: and they that love it shall eat the fruit thereof."*

You are foolish if you think you can speak and act any way you want and not suffer the consequences. As Christians, God expects you to *be* His through and through, and that means speaking, acting, believing—indeed, *living*—the Word of God.

As Elisha got ready to throw his stick in the water, another prophet stood by and watched. He probably thought, "There isn't a line or a hook on that stick. What is he doing? You can't fish with just a stick."

Elisha took the stick and threw it into the water anyway. When he did, the iron ax head floated to the surface. Imagine what must have happened in the heart of that other man!

Elisha said, "Here is the ax head. Take a look." Elisha faced his need with a spirit of faith. You can, too! God does not respond to worry and fear; the Bible says faith is what pleases the Lord and moves Him to action.

I can imagine the fish swimming in that part of the river that day. They watch a heavy object fall into the water and drop quickly to the bottom. Then, suddenly, the mud is stirred up and the ax head begins to move.

What happened? A law was broken—the law of gravity. God superseded the natural to meet the need of His prophet, and the ax head began to float to the surface. What brought the object to the top? Faith. The iron ax head floated, not just to the surface, but also to within the prophet's reach! God loves you. He wants to meet every need in your life. He does not just want to show you His faithfulness; He wants the blessings you need to be within your reach.

When you see God move, it stirs something inside you. You know His Word is true, and faith rises in your spirit. Take hold of the ax head! Receive God's provision for your life! Take it by faith and in so doing, you will shake the gates of hell.

The Battle Is Spiritual

Ephesians 6:10 says, *"Finally, my brethren, be strong in the Lord, and in the power of his might."* The earliest recorded Olympic Games took place in Greece. What happened to the losers? Their eyes were poked out.

In the next verse, Paul warns that you are not wrestling against flesh and blood. If you want to be free from the grip of poverty, you must realize you are fighting a spiritual battle. If you want to break the spirit of poverty in your mind, in your emotions, or your finances, see God as your Source.

God used Elisha mightily. He worked many miracles during his tenure as a prophet, yet he never lost sight of what was real and important. Second Kings 5 tells the story of Naaman, a respected captain of the Syrian army. Verse 1 says, *"Now Naaman, captain of the host of the king of Syria, was a great man with his master, and honorable, because by him the Lord had given deliverance unto Syria: he was also a mighty man in valour, but he was a leper."*

Naaman had everything: position, wealth, and honor; he was a mighty man of valor—but he was also a leper. Despite his success, he was physically impeded.

Still, perhaps because Naaman was a revered man of war, the king wanted a solution, a miracle of some kind. A Jewish servant girl told Naaman's wife about Elisha, and the wonders that God worked through him. She in turn told Naaman.

When the king heard the story, he collected what today would be tens of thousands in silver and gold and sent Naaman to see the prophet. He took with him a letter that commanded Elisha to heal the leprosy.

When Naaman arrived at Elisha's house, he waited for the prophet to come out and perform a miracle. But Elisha didn't come out. Instead, he sent a messenger to tell Naaman to wash in the Jordan River seven times. If he did so, Elisha said, the man would be healed.

Elisha would not take a dime from Naaman or the king. It was not that he did not need the money. The Bible says the prophet needed the finances to build a bigger school. Elisha was not swayed by money. He listened to the word of the Lord, and he obeyed. He did not "perform" for money. He offered healing and hope in the name of the Lord. Elisha trusted God to heal Naaman's leprosy and to meet his own needs.

Fear Not

When the leprous captain of the Syrian army came to Elisha for healing, the prophet said, "Fear not!"

When another one of the prophets lost a valuable iron ax head in the water, Elisha said, "Fear not!"

When he and his servant were surrounded by hostile, Syrian forces, Elisha said, "Fear not!"

Fear *is* a spirit, and unless you stand against it—and acknowledge God as your Source—the devil will use it to destroy your life.

A spirit of poverty will eat you alive if you allow it to. Find out what the Word of God says and walk in that truth! You don't have to be defeated by fear or poverty! The Bible says, *"The word is nigh thee, even in thy mouth, and in thy heart: that is, the word of faith, which we preach"* (Romans 10:8). Second Corinthians 4:18 says, *"While we look not at the things which are seen, but at the things which are not seen: for the things which are seen are temporal; but the things which are not seen are eternal."*

Why not acknowledge God as your Source right now—and break the spirit of poverty!

CHAPTER SEVENTEEN

Release Mustard Seed Faith

*Use your seed of faith to minister
to the needs of others.*

I f you are like most Christians, you want your faith to be effective. You want to see lives changed and Jesus glorified. You also want your faith to grow. You do not want to be stagnant and self-absorbed; you want your faith to be dynamic and uncompromising. That is good. That is what God wants for you, too!

So how do you develop effective, life-changing, dynamic faith? Where do you start? Jesus said you begin by planting your faith, as you plant a tiny seed.

Luke 17:5-6 says, *"And the apostles said unto the Lord, Increase our faith. And the Lord said, If ye had faith as a grain of mustard seed, ye might say unto this sycamine tree, Be thou plucked up by the root, and be thou planted in the sea; and it should obey you.*

The Root of the Problem

I once had a couple of pear trees, and one day I noticed the pears were falling off too soon. I started chasing the birds away because I thought they were eating the pears. Then, one morning I went outside and saw that the problem was not birds at all but a big, fat squirrel who was ravaging my pear trees!

When you are going through a tough time, you can direct your anger at the wrong person. You can unload on your spouse, your children, your boss, your parents, or your friends—and be absolutely mistaken in your efforts.

Ephesians 6:12 says, *"For we wrestle not against flesh and blood, but against principalities, against powers, against the rulers of the darkness of this world, against spiritual wickedness in high places."*

Your spouse is not really the problem. Neither are your children. You are under spiritual attack, and until you get to the *root* of the problem, the attack will continue. Mark 11:12-14 tells of a time Jesus was on His way home from Bethany. He was hungry and saw a fig tree in bloom: It was a bit early for the tree to be sprouting leaves but since the tree was in bloom, there was the promise of fruit. When He got closer, however, He saw that there was no fruit, so He cursed the tree.

Verse 20 says, *"And in the morning, as they passed by, they saw the fig tree dried up from the roots."* Why did the tree dry up from the roots? It is because the roots supplied the life to the tree. When you are dealing with a problem, you must get to the root if you want to see results; otherwise, the problem continues to grow.

When Jesus spoke to the tree, it died. When you want to overcome a problem, you must speak the Word of God.

The disciples heard Jesus curse the tree, but it took a while before they saw the results. The roots had to dry up before the tree withered at the top. Likewise, you may have to wait a while before you see the effect of the Word on your problem, but do not give up! Stand on the Word. Believe it! Declare its truth in your life.

Verses 21-24 say, *"And Peter calling to remembrance saith unto him, Master, behold, the fig tree which thou cursed is withered away. And Jesus answering saith unto them, Have faith in God. For verily I say unto you, That whosoever shall say unto this mountain, Be thou removed, and be thou cast in to the sea; and shall not doubt in his heart, but shall believe that those things which he saith shall come to pass; he shall have whatsoever he saith. Therefore I say unto you, What things soever ye desire, when ye pray, believe that ye receive them, and ye shall have them."*

Jesus said you could move mountains if you believe. He said you could curse the root of your problem and see it wither away—if you have faith.

Mark 9:17-27 tells the story of a desperate father who wanted Jesus to heal his son who was tormented by a "dumb spirit" that tore at him, made his mouth foam, and his teeth gnash. The spirit often threw the boy into fire and water to destroy him. The disciples tried to help but were powerless.

Jesus said the problem was their lack of faith. Verse 23 says, *"Jesus said unto him, If thou canst believe, all things are possible to him that believeth."*

Verse 24 says, *"And straightway the father of the child cried out, and said with tears, Lord, I believe; help thou mine unbelief."*

Jesus is not going to humiliate you when your faith is low. He wants to bolster your faith! When you are overwhelmed by the enemy, ask Jesus to increase your faith. You only need faith the size of a mustard seed to put the enemy to flight!

When the devil attacked our finances, we could have pleaded, cried, or begged, but we didn't. We listened to the Lord and obeyed His Word. The Spirit of God told me to start building people up, encouraging them, ministering to their hearts, and meeting their needs: He told me to trust Him and quietly do His will.

In time, we saw a release in our finances that only God could orchestrate. We also saw fruitfulness in the lives of those to whom we ministered. Because we sowed to the Spirit, we reaped a bountiful, kingdom harvest.

The Keys to the Kingdom

The Jewish leaders had a habit of carrying keys everywhere they went. The keys represented various degrees they had earned, and the more degrees they had, the more keys they carried. The equivalent to a bachelor's degree, for instance, was represented by a small key; a master's degree was represented by a larger key, and so on.

The Jews were proud of their religious education, so they displayed the keys for all the community to see and admire. They hung them at their sides.

The keys brought the Jewish leaders a certain amount of respect. They also enabled the educated few to enter the synagogue and unlock the Scriptures.

With a small key, they could read from the Psalms. Having a small key meant having a little authority. With a larger key, they could read from the Minor Prophets; with a big, granddaddy key, they could unlock the scrolls of Isaiah or the Major Prophets.

The Jews literally carried their authority with them. They held up their keys and bragged about their education. But Jesus wasn't the least bit impressed.

In Matthew 23:27-28, He said, *"Woe unto you, scribes and Pharisees, hypocrites! for ye are like unto whited sepulchers, which indeed appear beautiful outward, but are within full of dead men's bones, and of all uncleanness. Even so ye also outwardly appear righteous unto men, but within ye are full of hypocrisy and iniquity."*

In Luke 11:52, Jesus said, *"Woe unto you, lawyers! for ye have taken away the key of knowledge: ye entered not in yourselves, and them that were entering in ye hindered."*

Then, He did a remarkable thing. In Matthew 16:19, He said:

"And I will give unto thee the keys of the kingdom of heaven: and whatsoever thou shalt bind on earth shall be bound in heaven: and whatsoever thou shalt loose on earth shall be loosed in heaven."

The word "key" is very interesting. It is used only a few times in the Scriptures. In the Old Testament, the Hebrew word is "*maphteach,*" which means "an opener." It comes from the root word "*pathach,*" which means "to open wide, to loosen, to break forth, to draw out, to let go free."

In the New Testament, the Greek word for "key" is "*kleis,*" and it means "to lock." It is from the root word "*kleio,*" which means "*to close, or shut up.*"

Isaiah 22:22 says, *"And the key of the house of David will I lay upon his shoulder; so he shall open, and none shall shut; and he shall shut, and none shall open."*

Revelation 1:18 tells us, *"I am he that liveth, and was dead; and, behold, I am alive for evermore, Amen; and have the keys of hell and of death."*

Revelation 3:7 says, *"And to the angel of the church in Philadelphia write: These things saith he that is holy, he that is true, he that hath the key of David, he that openeth, and no man shutteth; and shutteth, and no man openeth;"*

Jesus has the power and authority to release blessings in your life. He has the power to set you free, and draw you out to do His will. Jesus has the keys that can lock up hell and death! Whatever He opens remains open, and whatever He closes, remains closed!

What is more, He has given *you* His authority to bind and loose, to lock and unlock blessings and curses, forgiveness and judgment, in His name!

You have the keys to the kingdom. What will you do with them? Will you set people free in the name of Jesus? Will you bless others? The choice is yours.

Faith that Grows

Second Thessalonians 1:3 says, *"We are bound to thank God always for you, brethren, as it is meet, because that your faith groweth exceedingly, and the charity of every one of you all toward each other aboundeth."*

You don't increase your faith by focusing your attention and energies on yourself. If you continue to walk in fear, to criticize others, to indulge in self-pity, you won't increase your faith one bit. You will only make your situation seem worse than it really is. The only way your faith will grow is if you walk in obedience to God and love toward one another.

Luke 13:18-19 says, *"Then said he, Unto what is the kingdom of God like? and whereunto shall I resemble it? It is like a grain of mustard seed, which a man took, and cast into his garden; and it grew, and waxed a great tree; and the fowls of the air lodged in the branches of it."*

Jesus compared the kingdom of God to a tiny mustard seed. He said it begins as a small, almost imperceptible thing, and grows, largely unseen, until it emerges as a strong tree.

Your faith is like that mustard seed. There may be times when you just do not think you have enough faith to do what God wants you to do. You do not think you have the faith to love that annoying person God has put in your life. You do not think you have the faith to pray and see mountainous problems cast into the sea.

That is when your faith is at its best! That is when God steps in and strengthens you by *His* power. That is when your faith is stretched beyond natural limits.

When you think you cannot rise to the occasion, you are in the perfect position to see God move on your behalf. Paul said in 2 Corinthians 12:9, *"And he said unto me, My grace is sufficient for thee: for my strength is made perfect in weakness...."*

A Faith That Overcomes

Let me ask you a few questions:

1. Where does faith come from? Most people think faith comes from reading the Bible. The Bible doesn't say that faith comes from reading the Bible. It says it comes from *hearing* the Word of God.

   Why does hearing the Word cause your faith to grow? Because the Word is powerful; it cuts through the chaff and exposes your heart to the light of God.

   Hebrews 4:12 says, *"For the word of God is living and active and sharper than any two-edged sword, and piercing as far as the division of soul and spirit, of both joints and marrow, and able to judge the thoughts and intentions of the heart."*

   The kind of hearing that builds faith is not merely a physical act; it is far more than hearing with your ears. In fact, it is entirely possible to hear with your ears but *not* with your heart. Matthew 13:13 says, *"Therefore I speak to them in parables: because they seeing see not; and hearing they hear not, neither do they understand."*

   When your heart hears the Word, you are stirred deep within your soul. You are challenged and changed and conformed by the Spirit of God. That is one reason it is so important to speak the Word.

   You release the power of God in your life every time your mouth agrees with your heart, and that power will destroy the works of the devil.

2. Where is your faith right now? Is it in your employer? You went to work for someone who probably did not show you his financial statement. You had no guarantee that there was money in the bank to pay your check.

   But you *believed* there would be money to cover your check.

You had faith in your employer and his ability to meet your financial needs.

Do you have the same faith in God? He is your Source. He has everything you need. Are you trusting Him, or are you putting your faith in people? If your trust is in men, you will be disappointed because they will fail you repeatedly. But God never fails.

As a Christian, you are commanded to draw near to Jesus. Your heart is to be clean and full of faith so you can hold onto the promises of God. Hebrews 10:22-23 says, *"Let us draw near with a true heart in full assurance of faith, having our hearts sprinkled from an evil conscience, and our bodies washed with pure water. Let us hold fast the profession of our faith without wavering; (for he is faithful that promised)."*

When your faith is weak look to Jesus. Hebrews 12:2 tells us He is the Author and Finisher of your faith!

3. What are you doing with your faith? Are you exercising it? If you want to have strong faith, you must exercise it, just as you exercise your muscles to make them strong. Use your faith. Obey the Word. When everyone else says, "Don't listen to God. He's telling you to do something impossible," trust the Lord to make it possible in your life.

    Are you sowing seeds of faith? If you want your faith to grow, you must plant it wherever God tells you to. Do not be intimated. Your faith might seem small, but it can still release the power of God. That is the secret of the mustard seed. Although it seems insignificant, there is enormous potential inside!

The kingdom of God is a kingdom where needs are met. There is *abundance* in the kingdom: abundance of grace, love, joy, provision, health, deliverance, life. God wants to bless you, but He wants *you* to be a channel of blessing to other people in the name of Jesus.

The Jesus You Need

Romans 10:17, "*So then faith cometh by hearing, and hearing but the word of God.*"

Hearing what? The Word of God. The Word you need.

Revelation 19:11-13 says, "*And I saw heaven opened, and behold a white horse; and he that sat upon him was called Faithful and True, and in righteousness he doth judge and make war. His eyes were as a flame of fire, and on his head were many crowns; and he had a name written, that no man knew, but he himself. And he was clothed with a vesture dipped in blood: and his name is called The Word of God.*"

Jesus is the *rhema*, or revealed Word of God. In Him, all your needs are met He is faithful and true. He is just and holy. He is the King of kings, and Lord of lords. He is your Savior, Deliverer, Master, and Friend, the Lover of your soul. Jesus is all you will ever need.

The Bible lists over two hundred names for God! These names reveal His character and nature. Here are a few examples. Notice how they are first declared in the Old Testament, and later affirmed in the New Testament.

1. Jehovah Jireh: Your Provider

    Genesis 22:8; 13-14 says, "*And Abraham said, My son, God will provide himself a lamb for a burnt offering: so they went both of them together. And Abraham lifted up his eyes, and looked, and behold behind him a ram caught in a thicket by his horns: and Abraham went and took the ram, and offered him up for a burnt offering in the stead of his son. And Abraham call the name of that place Jehovah Jireh: as it is said to this day, In the mount of the Lord it shall be seen.*"

    John 1:29 says, "*The next day John seeth Jesus coming unto him, and saith, Behold the Lamb of God, which taketh away the sin of the world.*"

2. Jehovah Shalom: Your Peace

Judges 6:22-24 says, "*And when Gideon perceived that he was an angel of the Lord, Gideon said, Alas, 0 Lord God[1] for because I have seen an angel of the Lord face to face. And the Lord said unto him, Peace be unto thee; fear not: thou shalt not die. Then Gideon built an altar there unto the Lord, and called it Jehovah- shalom: unto this day it is yet in Ophrah of the Abiezrites.*"

Ephesians 2:14-16 says, "*For he is our peace, who hath made both one, and hath broken down the middle wall of partition between us; Having abolished in his flesh the enmity, even the law of commandments contained in ordinances; for to make in himself of twain one new man, so making peace; And that he might reconcile both unto God in one body by the cross, having slain the enmity thereby.*"

3. Jehovah Tsidkenu: Your Righteousness

    Leviticus 11:45 says, "*For l am the Lord that bringeth you up out of the land of Egypt, to be your God: ye shall therefore be holy, for I am holy.*"

    Second Corinthians 5:21 says, "*For he hath made him to be sin for us, who knew no sin; that we might be made the righteousness of God in him.*"

4. Jehovah Rophe: Your Healer

    Psalm 103:2-3 says, "*Bless the Lord, 0 my soul, and forget not all his benefits: Who forgiveth all thine iniquities; who healeth all thy diseases.*"

    First Peter 2:24 says, "*Who his own self bare our sins in his own body on the tree, that we, being dead to sins, should live unto righteousness: by whose stripes ye were healed.*"

5. Jehovah Nissi: Your Standard

    Exodus 17:13-15 says, "*And Joshua discomfited the Amalek and his people with the edge of the sword. And the Lord said unto Moses, Write this for a memorial in a book, and rehearse it in the ears of Joshua: for I will utterly put out the remembrance of*

Amalek from under heaven. And Moses built an altar, and called the name of it Jehovah-nissi."

John 12:32 says, *"And if I be lifted up from the earth, will draw all men unto me."*

6. Jehovah Shammah: The Presence of God in Your Life

    Psalm 139:7-12 says, *"Whither shall I go from thy spirit? or whither shall I flee from thy presence? If I ascend up into heaven, thou art there: if I make my bed in hell, behold, thou art there. If I take the wings of the morning, and dwell in the uttermost parts of the sea; Even there shall thy hand lead me, and thy right hand shall hold me. If I say, Surely the darkness shall cover me; even the night shall be light about me. Yea, the darkness hideth not from thee; but the night shineth as the day: the darkness and the light are both alike to thee."*

    Matthew 28:20 says, *"Teaching them to observe all things whatsoever I have commanded you: and, lo, I am with you alway, even unto the end of the world. Amen. "*

7. Jehovah M'Kaddesh: Your Sanctification

    Leviticus 20:7-8 says, *"Sanctify yourselves therefore, and be ye holy: for I am the Lord your God. And ye shall keep my statutes, and do them: I am the Lord which sanctify you."*

    Ephesians 4:24 says, *"And that ye put on the new man, which after God is created in righteousness and true holiness."*

8. Jehovah Kohi: Your Shepherd

    Psalm 23:1 says, *"The Lord is my shepherd; I shall not want."*

    John 10:11 says, *"I am the good shepherd: the good shepherd giveth his life for the sheep."*

Where are you hurting today? Will you let Jesus manifest His character and nature in your life, and meet you at your deepest point of need?

Believe the Word

The first thing you need to do is to hear the Word. Receive it in the name, the authority, and the character of Jesus. Believe the Word of God. Declare the Word and exercise your faith.

Hebrews 11:1 says, "Now faith is the substance of things hoped for, the evidence of things not seen." *Second Corinthians 4:18 says,* "While we look not at the things which are seen, but at the things which are not seen: for the things which are seen are temporal; but the things which are not seen are eternal." *Second Corinthians 5:7 says,* "For we walk by faith, not by sight."

How are you walking today? Are you walking by sight? What should you do if you are ill? Deny the illness? No. The Bible does not say if you are sick, you should say you are not. God knows that you are sick. He doesn't want you to deny physical realities in your life; He does, however, want you to remember there is a higher reality, a kingdom reality.

He is saying, "Do not give sickness lordship over your life. Allow the mustard-seed principle to work. Allow My powerful, authoritative, creative Word to do its work in you. Speak the Word—and stand on its truth."

Fearless Faith

Luke 7:2-17 tells the story of a Roman centurion whose faith impressed Jesus. He had a favorite slave who was very sick, and in fact, dying. As soon as he heard about Jesus, the centurion sent some Jewish elders to ask Jesus to come and save the life of his slave. The elders told Jesus how important the centurion was. "He is highly respected in this area," they said. "He even built our synagogue for us!"

Jesus agreed to go, but before He reached the house, the centurion sent friends out to meet Him. They had a message for Jesus. In verses

6-8, the centurion says, *"...Lord, trouble not thyself: for I am not worthy that thou shouldest enter under my roof: Wherefore neither thought I myself worthy to come unto thee: but say in a word, and my servant shall be healed. For I also am a man set under authority, having under me soldiers, and I say unto one, Go, and he goeth; and to another, Come, and he cometh; and to my servant, Do this, and he doeth it."*

The centurion was well respected, honored by political and religious leaders alike. He was praised for his good deeds. Yet, he refused to put his faith in the words of men. He knew he was not as wonderful as everyone thought he was. He was just a man.

Jesus, on the other hand, was the Son of God. The centurion recognized His importance and gave all honor to Him. If you want Jesus to meet your needs, you must humble yourself before Him. Pride will get you nothing.

The centurion also recognized Jesus' authority over sickness. This man was a soldier, and he was used to giving orders. When he told someone to do something, he expected them to obey his word.

The same is true with Jesus. The difference, of course, was the degree of authority. The centurion had authority over the soldiers in his command and the servants in his house, but Jesus had absolute authority over sin, sickness, life, and death. The centurion knew that all Jesus had to do was say, "Go!" and the sickness had to leave. Jesus said He had never seen such faith!

Verse 9 says, *"When Jesus heard these things he marveled at him, and turned him about, and said unto the people that followed him, I say unto you, I have not found so great faith, no, not in Israel."*

How do you respond when there is a need in your life? Do you say, "God's Word is absolutely true, and I choose to believe it, no matter what"?

You do not have to be intimated by sickness. You don't have to be a slave to fear and doubt. Speak the Word, and see God move in your life!

Fear is the absence of faith. Just as darkness is the opposite of light and will leave as soon as you turn the light on, fear leaves as soon as you turn faith on. The moment faith is ignited, fear leaves.

You may not think your faith is big enough, or strong enough to drive the fear out of your life, but Jesus said all you need is faith the size of a mustard seed! It's not the size of your faith that matters, but *who* is behind it. Jesus is committed to finish what He started in your life. He is the Author and Finisher of your faith.

Faith will enable you to overcome any problem you might have. It will enable you to stand against the attack of the Enemy, and win, in Jesus' name! If you want to have overcoming faith, get hold of the mustard seed God has given you. Cast it into a garden and let it grow. Allow God to use your faith to set you free and then minister to others who are in bondage from fear.

CHAPTER EIGHTEEN

Celebrate Jesus

*Our preconceived image of Jesus doesn't even come
close to the real Jesus at His darkest hour.*

J esus entered Jerusalem on what we now call Palm Sunday.
Matthew 21:6-9 says, *"And the disciples went, and did as Jesus
commanded them, And brought the ass, and the colt, and put on
them their clothes, and they set him thereon. And a very great multitude
spread their garments in the way; others cut down branches from the
trees, and strewed them in the way. And the multitudes that went before,
and that followed cried, saying, Hosanna to the son of David: Blessed
is he who cometh in the name of the Lord; Hosanna in the highest."* In
Hebrew, that day is called the *Ho-sha-nach*, which means *"the branch."*
The palm or willow branch was a symbol of the Jews' deliverance
from slavery and their entrance into the Promised Land. When they
celebrated that day, they were really saying, "We were once slaves, but
we have been delivered from that and led into the Promised Land.
We are free!"

A Celebration of Faith

The Jews were afraid when they celebrated. They had tremendous fear. Why? Because in reality they were not truly free. In John 8:32, Jesus said, *"The truth shall make you free."* But the religious leaders responded by saying, "How can you talk to us about being free? We have never been in slavery!"

Jesus knew the Jews had been enslaved 26 times, and at that moment, they were under Roman rule! It is amazing how people who need to be set free can criticize someone who speaks the truth. You can be deceived. God help you to be humble and receptive to His Word!

Another reason the Jews were afraid was that they were commanded to pay their debts. All their vows and offerings were to be paid, and they were to be judged for their sins. The night before the feast was a horrible night for them because they believed that was when the book of death and life was opened. If they did not pay for their sins, they would be judged. It is sad, but many Believers often live like that—always trying to pay their debts to be good enough to escape judgment.

Nothing but Jesus

When the people came into Jerusalem, they waved their branches until every leaf fell off. The Jews beat the branches as a symbol of new life, pointing them in every direction—north, south, east and west.

I remember talking with an individual who wanted advice regarding a certain problem. I told him to pray, stand tight and to believe God.

No matter what your need is today, do not panic. If you are depending on religion to save you, or if you are looking to man for help—then you have a reason to panic. If God is your Source, and you really believe that He is on His throne and all the angels in heaven are at His disposal, then you can face your problem with confidence and faith. You do not have to give into fear and panic!

Be patient, pray, believe, trust, and look toward heaven. Look to the east, west, north, and south for a miracle. Look to Jesus. He alone can save.

Expect a Miracle

As Jesus entered Jerusalem, the Jews pointed their branches in all directions, but they did not really expect a miracle. They hailed Jesus as their new leader, but they had no idea He was the Messiah they sought. They expected an earthly king, not a sacrificial Lamb; they could not see that His kingdom was spiritual, not political. They wanted to be free from Roman rule, but they did not understand they were in spiritual bondage.

Fear and bondage to sin will make you settle for mediocrity. You will begin to believe that if you just make it through the next day, the next week, the next year, you will be all right. But that isn't living; that is merely surviving! If you want true freedom, you have to expect a miracle! Are you trying to be good enough to win God's approval? Are you trying to please men? Are you trying to find peace on your own? Are you doing whatever it takes to make it through another week?

Stop and reconsider Jesus! Acknowledge Him afresh as your Messiah. Let Him rule your heart and life.

You can be free from fear! You can be an overcomer! You don't have to live in bondage to sin! You can be free to celebrate *real* Life in Jesus!

The Gospel of Deliverance

God says to each of us, "Let Me deliver you from the sin that entangles you. I have something better for you. Trust Me."

The gospel of Jesus is not a gospel for people who want to maintain a prisoner mentality. It is a gospel that *delivers* captives and sets them *free*—once and for all through the power of His blood.

You are not simply a "saved sinner," you are a new creation in Jesus! You have been pardoned! Your sins have been removed "as far as the east is from the west."

Priest and a Lamb

First Peter 2:9 says, *"But ye are a chosen generation, a royal priesthood, an holy nation, a peculiar people; that ye should shew forth the praises of him who hath called you out of darkness into his marvelous light."* Before the feast could begin, the high priest had to prepare himself, the temple, and the people. First, he sacrificed a bullock every day for several days prior to the celebration. He also performed various ceremonial rituals. While the priest cleansed the temple and the instruments to be used in worship, the people marched around the altar.

The Bible says Jesus is our High Priest, but are you trying to do His job? Are you trying to "cleanse the temple" within your heart? Are you trying to *do* something that will make you acceptable to God? Are you offering your own sacrifices? Are you going through religious motions in the hope that you will find freedom and peace?

Remember, Jesus *is* your High Priest. He is also the sacrificial Lamb. You do not need to do anything to be acceptable to God. Jesus has done it all—on your behalf! You just need to put your faith in Him and accept His finished work!

Choose the Right Altar

So many people, including some Christians, are marching around fleshly altars today. They devote their time and energies to the pursuit of things, to improved houses, to faster, sleeker cars, to careers, to fame, to countless activities that exclude the Lord, but when the fire of God comes, all those *things* that seemed so important burn to ashes.

That is why people fall apart in times of crisis. They have identified themselves with what they *do* or what they *have,* and when those things are gone, so is their reason for being.

They do not know that Jesus is their Source for everything they need: their identity, their happiness, their peace, their health, their physical needs, and their sanity—their life!

When the fire rages, you find out quickly who your source is. Around which altar are you marching today? Choose the right altar, the altar of God! No matter what your need, God is your Source! If you do not know whom you are, apart from what you do or what you own, He is your Identity. If you are sick, He is your Healer. If you are caught in the grip of fear and sin, remember: He is able to deliver you!

The crisis of the Church in the 21th century is not carnality in the pulpit, but a lack of confidence in Jesus in the pew.

Will you allow the fire of God to cleanse, purge, and fill your heart with joy, power, and peace? You must not only march around the altar of God; you must get to the fire.

"Thou Art My God"

During the feast, the people sang a number of Psalms, from 113 through 118. Psalm 118:27b-28 says, *"...bind the sacrifice with cords, even unto the horns of the altar. Thou art my God, and I will praise thee: thou art my God, I will exalt thee."* They sang a Psalm that prophesied the Lord's death and resurrection!

That should have been the finest hour for God's covenant people! It should have been the moment that all eyes were turned, not toward oxen or bullocks, priests or temples, but toward Jesus, the Lamb of God!

Do you realize that the Church of Jesus Christ at its very worst is far better than the world at its best? Before you allow bitterness, condemnation, judgment, or strife to rule your heart, examine the cross of Christ. You dare not move anywhere except through the altar and the blood of Jesus.

Power in the Blood

The day of the feast was a day to celebrate. Indeed, it was a very special day for the people of God. The priest held a golden pitcher that he filled with water from the pool of Siloam. That water was poured over the altar; then, it flowed from a drain down to the Eastern Gate.

The Jews believed that the water from the Pool of Siloam would deliver someone from something. However, they did not know that someone was about to step onto the scene who would say, "Drink of Me. I have water that will satisfy your soul, and you will never thirst again. That water is My blood, and it will set captives free."

Freedom in Jesus

The children of Israel went through their various rituals. They blew the shofar. The Levites sang praises to the Lord. "Our eyes are upon the Lord," they declared.

Later in the night, they took torches and danced as they headed toward the Eastern Gate to celebrate their atonement and deliverance.

You know when a person is free. You do not have to prophesy about it or talk about it. You can look into his eyes and see the fruit of his freedom.

If you are brokenhearted, turn to Jesus. When you have nothing left, turn to Him. Only then will you find real—and lasting—freedom.

A Just King

Zechariah 9:9 says, *"Rejoice greatly, 0 daughter of Zion; shout, 0 daughter of Jerusalem: behold, thy King cometh unto thee: he is just, and having salvation; lowly, and riding upon an ass, and upon a colt the foal of an ass."* God says He is just. You want justice in your marriage, your business, with your children, and even with those who do not like you. But God says He is just, so if you want justice, follow Him.

He is the One who will bring you justice! That is His response to the injustice of the world. His response to pain and injustice is simply this: "I forgive you."

Jesus interrupted the Jews' celebration and, at first, it made them angry. Nevertheless, they got their eyes off Man, the traditions of Man, the opinions of Man, and they said, "Let's go and see the deliverer."

They went, and a wonderful thing happened: they began to worship Jesus! They sang their Hosannas to the King of kings. They celebrated Jesus—and glorified Him as He entered the city of Jerusalem.

Imagine how exciting it must have been! There was Jesus, entering the City of David, flanked on every side by men, women, and children who shouted their praises to God.

Yet, the day in which we live is even more exciting because the King of kings lives within us! Soon, we will see His glorious return!

Jesus Took the Cup

After the celebration, Jesus left the city and headed in a different direction. He went to pray in the Garden of Gethsemane. When He arrived, He sat by a rock and a huge, old olive tree; there, our Lord knelt with a cup in His hand.

In those days, and today as well, devout Jews wore prayer shawls. The tassels on the ends of the shawl symbolized the Word of God.

Mark 5:25- 34 tells the story of a sick woman who believed that if she touched the hem of Jesus' garment, she would be healed—and she was! When she reached out to touch the hem of Jesus' garment, she was reaching out for the Word of God, the Living Word.

You don't need to reach for those tassels anymore—because He shed His *blood* for you! Jesus took the cup as he knelt in the garden, and He saw you and all of your sins.

He had a choice. He could take into His own body *your* sins, or He could set that cup aside. His struggle was so great that the Bible says He sweat great drops of blood.

Many doctors believe that subcutaneous blood vessels ruptured. Psychologists will tell you that under great physiological pressure, this can happen. The blood was pouring out right through his pores.

The Way, the Truth, and the Life

Jesus faced incredible stress and personal pain while obeying the Father. He would take the sin of the world into Himself and go to the cross with it. He determined to do this while you were still in sin!

He was not going to wait until you were good enough! He was not going to wait until you found some other way of redemption! There was no other way!

In Matthew 26:42, He said, *"O my Father, if this cup may not pass away from me, except I drink it, thy will be done."*

Jesus sets a lost and dying world free!

Some people go through all sorts of religious rituals to "honor" Jesus, but in truth, they do not believe He can set them free. That is partly because they have a preconceived idea of who Jesus is. He isn't the revealed Word of God but the product of their own minds, and that "image" says they are powerless to change. They will always be in bondage to sin. They will always live in fear. They have been hurt, so they have the right to judge, condemn, and reject others.

However, that preconceived image of Jesus does not even come close to the real Jesus at His darkest hour. The real Jesus was wounded for our transgressions and bruised for our iniquities. He endured the humiliation and agony of the cross so you could be free.

He is the King of kings, and the Lord of lords! He is our Savior and our Deliverer! He is the Lamb who takes away the sin of the world! He is our interceding, faithful High Priest! He is the Messiah! He is the Way, the Truth, and the Life!

What better reason to celebrate Jesus!

CHAPTER NINETEEN

Accept the Atonement

When Jesus died, He finished the work that was
started by Old Testament Law—and now, you can
enter into His Sabbath rest!

Every year, the Jews celebrate a very special holiday, called Yom Kippur, or the "Day of Judgment." They also refer to it as the "Seventh Day." We call it the "Day of Atonement." For Jews, the day is a reminder that God is just, and that He judges sin. For us, it is a reminder that Jesus is the sacrificial Lamb of God, and that He is returning soon. Leviticus 16 says the children of Israel were required to do certain things to celebrate the Day of Atonement.

First, they blew the *shofar* as a sign that God had heard their prayers. On Yom Kippur, a Jewish man might go to the synagogue and ask the rabbi if his sins had been forgiven. The rabbi would reply, "Who knows?" Hebrews 9:12-14 assures us that God does indeed forgive sin! *"Neither by the blood of goats or calves, but by His own blood. He entered in once into the holy place, having obtained eternal redemption for us. For if the blood of bulls and of goats, and the ashes of an heifer sprinkling the unclean, sanctifieth to the purifying of the flesh:*

How much more shall the blood of Christ, who through the eternal Spirit offered Himself without spot to God purge your conscience from dead works to serve the living God?"

The Bible says that without the shedding of blood, there is no remission, or forgiveness, of sin. That is precisely why Jesus *had* to die. Throughout His entire life, Jesus obeyed the Father. He was tempted like you are, but He never succumbed to temptation. As a man, He understood your weaknesses, and He showed you how to walk in liberty and intimacy with God.

When Jesus died, He took our sin, *your* sin, into His own body. He took all your rebellion and pride, your unbelief and fear, your selfishness and your secrecy—He took *all* of it into Himself. He also took your *tendency* to sin; that is, your fleshly nature. The Bible says Jesus *became* sin that He might render it powerless by His blood and resurrection. Second Corinthians 5:21 says, *"For he hath made him to be sin for us, who knew no sin; that we might be made the righteousness of God in him."*

Jesus' death on the cross guaranteed our freedom from sin. His shed blood ensured our liberation from fear and oppression. That is why atonement comes *only* by the blood of Jesus, or as Hebrews 10:20 says, by a "new and *living* way," The Bible says, *"Seeing then that we have a great high priest, that is passed into the heavens, Jesus the Son of God, let us hold fast our profession."* (Hebrews 4:14).

A Symbol of Forgiveness

Devout Jews do not eat with anyone who is not in fellowship with the Lord. Eating food together is a sign of forgiveness. In other words, you never eat with an enemy.

Sharing a meal is more than an act of hospitality. If you eat with someone, you are one with that person—you are not just filling your stomach. That is why the children of Israel spent so much time in fellowship with one another, particularly around the table—it was a symbol of forgiveness.

Remember when the prodigal son returned home? The first thing the father did was to have the fatted calf killed and to order a great celebration. Why? Because the father had forgiven his son!

His brother was so angry he refused to come inside and eat with everyone else. He objected when his father gave the prodigal a ring and a robe, but he could not eat with someone he had not forgiven.

Peter experienced this symbol of forgiveness, too. When the soldiers arrested Jesus, the disciples fled. Peter, on the other hand, followed Jesus and waited outside the high priest's courtyard. He wanted to know what was happening to His master. When someone identified him and questioned his relationship with Jesus, Peter denied he had ever known Him. Three times Peter denied the Lord.

It was a terrible moment for Peter and when it was all over, he went back to his fishing boat; he had had enough. But as they drifted along, they heard someone call to them. Somewhere out on the beach, a familiar voice encouraged the men to cast their nets on the other side of the boat. Peter recognized the voice of Jesus; he jumped in the water and swam to the shore. As soon as Jesus saw him, He invited Peter to come have breakfast. Peter had been forgiven!

Atonement In Jesus

Through the atonement, God is calling us back to His *shabbat* rest. He is calling *you* to rest in Him and His finished work on the cross. He knows you have been harassed, and He sees how preoccupied you are. Now, He invites you to come and rest your weary soul. "Step away from the rat-race," He says, "and receive revelation knowledge."

The word "atonement" means "a covering or, to cover." It is used 77 times in the Old Testament, but it is never used in the New Testament in quite the same sense. The atonement in the New Testament is more than just a doctrine—it is the Body of Jesus.

"Atonement" can be explained as "at-one-ment" with God. Jesus died so your broken relationship with the Father could be restored, and the basis for your restoration is rest. You are invited to rest in the finished work of Jesus.

In the Garden of Eden, God *commanded* Adam and Eve to rest. God Himself had set the standard: He worked for six days and then rested on the seventh. When you are "at one" with the Father, you are at rest.

The Tabernacle in You

In Exodus 35 through 38, we read about the tabernacle. One thing is certain: it was a remarkable sight! The tabernacle of God contained three and three-fourths tons of gold—*over 7,000 pounds!* It was comprised of two-and-a-half tons of silver.

The construction cost tens of millions of dollars. One lamp stand alone, in our day, would be worth $500,000. Yet, that tabernacle was merely a *shadow* of what was to come. The tabernacle God was interested in inhabiting was the tabernacle of the heart. Think about it! Your spirit is God's dwelling place! That is what the Word says.

First Peter 1:18-19 says, *"Forasmuch as ye know that ye were not redeemed with corruptible things, such as silver and gold, from your vain conversation received by tradition from your fathers; But with the precious blood of Christ, as of a lamb without blemish and without spot."*

The Old Testament tabernacle was beautiful and very costly, but God said it was *nothing* compared to the tabernacle in you! Every year, the people went to the tabernacle to find cleansing and forgiveness for their sin. The priests and the people alike worked hard to secure God's atonement, but it was only temporary. It was not enough to save and deliver.

When Jesus died, He *finished* the work that was started by Old Testament Law—and now, *you* can enter into His Sabbath rest!

Old Covenant Requirements

Leviticus 16 explains the procedures that the Old Testament Law required to atone for sin:

1. The high priest had to pay a penalty if he went into the holiest part of the Tabernacle on any other day. If the priest went into the holy of holies on any day except the Day of Atonement, he died. But because of the shed blood of Jesus, you can have atonement for your sin 365 days a year.

2. The people had to bring a sin offering as well as a burnt offering. They had to hunt for those sacrificial offerings on the same day. Jesus, the Lamb of God, was both of those offerings.

3. Aaron had to lay aside his garments before he entered the holy of holies. This has meaning for you today, because you must also lay aside your "garments" of works and self-righteousness. You cannot go to God clothed in anything except the blood and righteousness of Jesus.

4. The blood of slain bullocks and goats had to be taken into the holy of holies and sprinkled on the mercy seat. Remember when Jesus told Mary, "Do not touch Me, for I must ascend to My Father"? He had to present *His* blood to the Father.
    What a spectacular day that must have been! Jesus, ascending into heaven, surrounded by angels. How they must have marveled to see Him bring His own blood to the Father as the sacrifice for sin!

5. Aaron took the golden censer, full of burning coals from the altar, with sweet incense that had been beaten—and the smoke went up to the Lord and covered the mercy seat.

In Leviticus 1 and 2, we read that Aaron's two sons died when they put fire instead of burning coals into the censer. The Bible says they offered "strange fire" unto the Lord. They did away with the mercy seat. They decided it was enough to go through the motions, but they were wrong, and they paid with their lives.

That is also why the fire that moved in both the Jesus movement of the 60's and the Charismatic movement of the 70's died. People were offering up unholy fire.

They thought they could live any way they wanted and still be considered holy. They thought they could go through the motions and satisfy the Lord. However, they were wrong, and the anointing left them. You cannot play games with the Holy Spirit.

6. The high priest went alone into the holy of holies. You have an Advocate and High Priest—Jesus—who continually intercedes for you before the Father.

7. Seven days before the priest entered the holy of holies, he had to separate himself from everyone else. Then, when he went in, he had to sprinkle blood on the horns of the altar. By removing himself from the other priests and the people, he entered into *God's* rest. You enter that rest through Jesus.

Another interesting parallel is found in the Jewish wedding ritual. When a young man wants to marry a young woman, he goes to her and negotiates the price of the wedding. For us, this represents the blood of Jesus. Then, he returns to his father's house.

The bride does not know when he will come to her—she just has to be ready. When he comes, he sends the wedding guests ahead to shout, "The bridegroom cometh!" She prepares herself and goes with him to his father's house.

Then, for seven days, the couple consummates the marriage

before the groom presents his bride to the guests at the feast of celebration.

Think for a moment. How long is the tribulation? Seven years. What will Jesus do during that time? He will take His bride. He will consummate the marriage. There will be a great feast—then, He will come back to show off His bride!

8. Every man had to present a ransom for his soul; he had to bring atonement money, or else plagues would be visited upon him. Before the people could rest on this holy day, they had to provide wave or peace offerings.

    God does not do that to us. You are not judged by your works. You are judged by your faith in Jesus—or lack of it.

    You will not go home with leprosy if you fail to pay your tithes. You make yourself *vulnerable* to attacks from the enemy when you cheat God, but that is your doing, not God's. *You* give the devil permission to devour and consume everything you have.

    When you realize Jesus atoned for your sin, you are both blessed and protected. Jesus was the ransom God demanded for sin. Accept His finished work, and enter into His rest!

"Rejoice in the Lord"

One of the prisons where Paul was incarcerated was a dark hole, with barely enough room for forty-two prisoners. Those who received the death sentence knew they would be crucified, strangled, skinned alive, or beheaded. Only the Roman citizens were beheaded.

Imagine the apostle Paul, shackled, in a rat-infested cell, having food dumped down to him. He was surrounded by sin, death, and fear. However, in Philippians 4:4, he says, *"Rejoice in the Lord always: and again I say, Rejoice."*

Paul entered into the holy of holies, into God's rest. Can you imagine what the prisoners thought when they heard him say this? They were about to be skinned alive, crucified, strangled—or beheaded, if they were lucky. Then, in verse 8, Paul says, *"Finally, brethren, whatsoever things are true, whatsoever things are honest, whatsoever things are just, whatsoever things are pure, whatsoever things are lovely, whatsoever things are of good report, if there be any virtue; and if there be any praise, think on these things."*

If you took the time to memorize the book of Philippians and then meditated on its truth, you would be encouraged in every aspect of your life. If you *applied* its truth to your circumstances, you would overcome fear.

Jesus stripped away the power of sin, death, hell, and the grave when He entered into the holy of holies! He disarmed fear with His precious blood, and He set you free from its grip. Now, you can enter into His rest by accepting the reality of the Atonement.

CHAPTER TWENTY

Discover the Gladness of God

Some of the best jokes I ever heard, I heard from God!

The Bible talks a lot about joy because Christians are supposed to be happy people. The worst advertisement for Christianity is a Believer with a fearful and broken spirit. But, the good news is that you don't have to be afraid! You do not have to be down-hearted! An old hymn tells why: "On Christ, the solid Rock, I stand. All other ground is sinking sand." In addition, Psalm 118:22-24 says, *"The stone which the builders refused has become the head stone of the comer. This is the Lord's doing; it is marvelous in our eyes. This is the day which the Lord hath made; we will rejoice and be glad in it."*

Gladness Is a Choice

Notice the Scripture says, "We *will* be glad." Gladness is a choice! Like my daughter sometimes says, "You need to notify your face that Jesus is Lord!" You may feel you have reasons *not* to be glad. I had a reason one morning when I woke up very tired from a late night. In my haste, I grabbed what I thought was spray gargle, but I squirted deodorant into my mouth instead! When things like this—or much worse—happen, choose to say, "I will be glad in the Lord." You *can* develop a spirit of gladness and joy!

You see people everywhere who have joy—and many people who do not. What is the difference? Are some people just naturally more joyful? Are they born that way? Or, have they developed a joyful spirit by making wise choices in their lives?

Right Relationships

A spirit of gladness first comes with right relationships. Right relationships are not built quickly, and when there is a problem, they are not repaired with quick fixes. Relationships that honor God and produce joy take time and effort—but they are worth it!

In this day of instant everything, people often want deep relationships to happen overnight. People who do not know the Lord often look for intimacy at work, at the gym, in bars, or at parties. Even many Christians are guilty of this; the difference is that they usually look for intimacy at church. There is nothing wrong with developing relationships at work or at the gym or at church, of course, but intimacy *must* begin with Jesus. He must be *first* in your life. Otherwise, you enter a relationship with false expectations and unrealistic goals.

If you are not whole, your tendency will be to look for someone who can complete you. The only Person who can bring completion to your life is Jesus! That is why He must be the focus of your life and your relationships. Healthy relationships are a lot of work. Why? Because you have two people with individual opinions, tastes, personal histories, goals, and desires to consider. Each person brings something unique to the relationship: talents, experiences, a sense of humor, and expectations all contribute to the depth and quality of a relationship.

When God is given *first* place in the relationship, those qualities are viewed through *His* eyes. Each characteristic is appreciated for what it is—an expression of Jesus in the individual's life.

In those areas where there is a need for growth and change, God is given room to move. His authority is recognized and welcomed. A couple, whose relationship is submitted to the lordship of Jesus, cannot help but experience joy and a sense of fulfillment!

When there is conflict, it is resolved in a way that pleases the Lord and produces greater intimacy. You do not develop gladness and joy by blowing up at a person whenever he makes a mistake. You must learn to turn the situation over to the Lord.

Pray this way: "God, Your Word says love never fails. It says love is not easily provoked, and it does not take into account a wrong suffered. It says love is patient and kind. Love does not rejoice in unrighteousness, but rejoices with the truth. It says love bears all things, believes all things, hopes all things, and endures all things. I love this person, and I know You love him, too; therefore, I choose to respond in a way that is loving."

I heard someone say one time, "It is more important to love than it is to be right." People who have critical spirits do not have joy, no matter how much truth they have. Conversely, people who love have an abundance of joy, even when they make a mistake!

Joy in the Lord

Psalm 64:10 says, *"The righteous shall be glad in the Lord, and shall trust in him; and all the upright in heart shall glory."*

God wants us to be in a right relationship with the Him first, and then develop right relationships with each other. That produces joy. It changes us inside.

Psalm 47:1 says, *"O clap your hands, all ye people; shout unto God with the voice of triumph."*

Psalm 98:8 says, *"Let the floods clap their hands: let the hills be joy-*

ful together before the Lord."

Psalm 63:4 says, *"Thus will I bless thee while I live: I will lift up my hands in thy name."*

Repeatedly, the Bible says you are to relate to God with joy. Why? Because joy is a spiritual force. It is not only powerful but also necessary for the health of your relationships. However, it does not always come naturally.

Many Christians have allowed fear to keep them from a life of joy and peace. They are so serious about themselves! They are afraid of everything. They do not really believe God is a good God who loves them and wants to pour out His blessings.

They focus their attention on their problems, not on the Word. They have forgotten how to trust the Lord. They have forgotten how to pray. They have forgotten how to laugh. Do you know some of the best jokes I ever heard, I heard from God?

Attack of the Sand Crabs

One night, my family and I were returning home from a crusade. We had been in Hawaii, and one of my girls had brought back six or eight medium-sized sand crabs. She had slipped them inside two paper cups without telling anyone.

When we got on the plane, she stuck them in the pouch behind the seat, and we all drifted off to sleep.

Suddenly, I was awakened by a woman's scream. I looked up and saw a sand crab crawling over the woman's shoulder! Another crab was running down the aisle as fast as it could go.

Still another had crawled onto a passenger. The whole plane was in a panic. We were chasing crabs all over the place. This experience might not have brought joy to anyone else, but it certainly did to us! It was downright funny!

Many people think that because they know Jesus, they automatically have joy. However, it does not work that way. Knowing Jesus Christ means you have the *basis* and *opportunity* for a life of joy. Unless you let Jesus reign in every area of your life, and you learn to laugh at your circumstances, you will not have a life of joy.

The Bible says the devil has come to steal, kill, and destroy. That is true. He wants to steal your joy, kill your faith, and destroy your life. But Jesus has also come—and in His goodness and grace, He offers you abundant life!

Horns of a Dilemma

You could be like the county agriculture extension agent from Texas who went out to visit an old farmer one day. He said, "I have a card here which gives me the authority to go through your farm and check everything out. If your place does not match up to our codes, I can shut you down. That's right; this card gives me the power to do whatever I want." The old man just looked at him and said, "Go on and exercise your rights, then. Take a look around."

The agent started going through the barns first. He came to a large red barn and asked, "What's in there?"

The farmer simply replied, 'You have the card and the authority. Go in and find out for yourself."

As it so happened, the farmer had a prize bull in that barn—a big, ornery fellow. When the man opened the gate, the bull bolted through it, and headed straight for the agent. "Help me!" he cried. "Make him stop!"

The old farmer just smiled and said, "Show him the card, son. Show him the card!"

As you can see, having a certain amount of authority did not help the county agent when he was facing the horns of a dilemma, so to speak. The same is true for you. Just because you have invited Jesus into your heart does not mean you are experiencing His joy. His grace and authority are yours for the asking. His blessings are yours as well. So is His joy—but you have to receive it!

Meditate on His Word

Psalm 104:34 says, *"My meditation of him shall be sweet: I will be glad in the-Lord."* The Bible says you need to *meditate* on Scripture. Why? Because God's Word is true and it never fails. It is full of wisdom and will instruct you in the way you should go and in the choices you should make. It will show you the Father's heart and help you understand His will for your life. It will cause your love for Jesus to grow. It will bring peace when your heart is full of fear and turmoil. It will help you remember that God is still in control, and He is working everything to your benefit.

Meditating on the Word will bring rest to your weary soul and body. Try this: before you close your eyes at night, read one or two verses. Let your mind *dwell* on them for 15 minutes or so—and see if your sleep is not sweet!

Psalm 32:11 says, *"Be glad in the Lord, and rejoice, ye righteous: and shout for joy, all ye that are upright in heart."*

Proverbs 15:13-15 says, *"A merry heart maketh a cheerful countenance: but by sorrow of the heart the spirit is broken. The heart of him that hath understanding seeketh knowledge: but the mouth of fools feedeth on foolishness. All the days of the afflicted are evil: but he that is of a merry heart hath a continual feast."*

Proverbs 17:22 says, *"A merry heart doeth good like a medicine: but a broken spirit drieth the bones."*

When the pressures of life weigh you down, meditate on the Word! When you are worried and full of fear, meditate on the Word!

God is still on His throne! His Word is true! Hebrews 4:12 says it is *"Quick, and powerful, and sharper than any two-edged sword, piercing even to the dividing asunder of soul and spirit, and of the joints and marrow, and is a discerner of the thoughts and intents of the heart."*

Focusing on your problems can make you forget that gladness, joy, and laughter can bring release and deliverance. Meditating on the Word of God puts everything in perspective. What a wonderful way to refresh your spirit and revitalize your joy!

You cannot lose your joy unless you *give* it to the thief. I do not care what anyone says; if you lose your joy, it is because you gave it to the devil!

Stop dwelling on your problems! Stop letting fear dictate your responses! Meditate on the Word instead—and release the joy of the Lord in your life!

On the Road to Damascus

Let me tell you one more story that makes me laugh. Some years ago, I hired a man named Charles West to produce television shows for me. He was both knowledgeable and creative, and he loved the Lord with all his heart. I enjoyed working with Charles, so I asked him to accompany me on a trip to Israel one time.

The only problem was that every time I looked for Charles, I could not find him.

For instance, we were supposed to go to Haifa and videotape some segments there, but Charles was nowhere to be found. He had simply disappeared. I could not find him anywhere.

Charles was so taken with Jerusalem that he "took off" for the city every chance he got! Each day became an adventure as I tried to track down my wandering friend.

One day Charles and I decided to go to Beirut. Charles wanted to drive, and I agreed. Everything was fine—for a while—until we realized we were not going toward Beirut at all; we were headed for Syria!

With every mile, the trip became more treacherous, and before long, we found ourselves smack in the middle of a war zone. We were driving as fast as we could go, trying to get back to Israel. Then, I saw a sign that said "Damascus"!

After a few bumps and turns, we made it back to the city and home to the hotel. Evidently, Charles' internal "radar" did not work outside the city of Jerusalem.

Let Faith Be Your Guide

When you are lost in the middle of a "war zone," put your faith in God and put a smile on your face! The Word of God will guide you home, and joy will follow.

Faith is a wonderful gift from the Lord. Use it!

Put your faith in the Holy Ghost, and He will bring laughter to your heart. Put your faith in the Lord and His ability to answer prayer, and you will find joy. Put your faith in the eternal promises of God, and gladness will replace fear and despair. Let faith be your guide and remember...God wants to give you a merry heart!

CHAPTER TWENTY-ONE

Destroy the Yoke

In the kingdom of God, there are no burden bearers
with broken backs.

I n my travels across America, I have met a surprising number of
Christians who are living defeated lives. They feel beaten down
by their circumstances. They are worried, fearful, sick and appear completely downcast. They are discouraged and filled, not with
faith, but with "doom and gloom." Their attention is focused on negative situations and as a result, they carry a heavy burden.

In talking with these brothers and sisters, I have discovered a
common thread: For the most part, they are not praying in the Spirit
or reading the Word. They are trying to carry the load by themselves,
and they are overwhelmed. Their burden is so great they almost believe they are beyond help. If you are one of these downcast Christians, I have good news for you today—God has joy equal to your
burden! You do not have to live in fear any longer. Joy can replace
fear!

The Yoke Shall Be Destroyed

Isaiah 10:27 says, *"And it shall come to pass in that day, that his burden shall be taken away from off thy shoulder and his yoke from off thy neck, and the yoke shall be destroyed because of the anointing."* If there is no anointing in your life, you will carry your burdens by yourself. No matter what you do, the weight you feel must be overwhelming. Take heart! God has promised to lift your burden because of the Spirit's anointing! Psalm 55:22 says, *"Cast thy burden upon the Lord, and he shall sustain thee: he shall suffer the righteous to be moved."* In Matthew 11:28 we read, *"Come unto me, all ye that labor and are heavy laden, and I will give you rest."*

The Bible is filled with stories about people who were loaded down with heavy burdens and to tell you the truth, I am glad God's Word is so candid about this subject. Frankly, we all have burdens to carry. Every day we face challenges to our health, finances, relationships, and our plans for the future. You have the opportunity to respond either positively or negatively to life's challenges. We can acknowledge the Lordship of Jesus and allow Him to use these experiences to help us grow spiritually—or we can ride an emotional merry-go-round and become blind, bitter, and spiritually bound.

When King David was in Ziklag, the city of despair, the Bible says he *"encouraged himself in the Lord."* That is very important. When you are dealing with a difficult situation, it is natural to want sympathy and support. If that does not come, the tendency is to feel sorry for yourself and to get upset—adding to your feelings of despair.

God's reality is greater than your circumstances. He will allow you to go through painful times because He wants to teach you something about His faithfulness and ultimately bless you. He has not turned His back on you. That is why it is so important to encourage yourself in the Lord—especially when you need joy and peace.

A Song in the Night

The apostle Paul had many burdens. The Bible says that one time he was beaten and thrown into a dark Philippian jail. He could have despaired, but he did not. Instead, he sang praises to God. From a natural perspective, Paul had nothing to sing about. Still, he understood something in the *Spirit realm* that was transforming, something that brought joy to his heart, *joy equal to his burden.* While he was singing, God shook the jail and touched the life of a frightened Philippian jailer.

After he was imprisoned in Rome, Paul wrote a letter to the Christians at Philippi. He said, *"Rejoice in the Lord, and again I say rejoice!"* No matter how bad his circumstances were, Paul knew that God would not forsake him; indeed, He would give him joy equal to his burden!

Then, there was John the Revelator, who eventually was boiled in oil. He spent his last years in a prison on a desolate island called Patmos. I have been on the isle of Patmos. I know what it looks like, and it is not even a nice place to visit. If anyone had a reason to despair, it was John, but he did not.

The Bible says John was in the Spirit on the Lord's Day when he received the revelation from Jesus. I believe Jesus decided to bless John in a remarkable way at least partly because John was encouraging himself in the Lord. He had refused to be defeated by his circumstances, and so he was given the greatest revelation about the end times anyone has ever received.

The Garden of the Lord

The Bible does not promise a quick fix for your problems. It does promise, however, that you will not face your problems alone. God knows you are living in a hostile world, and there will be times when you feel like you are fighting from a foxhole—but that does not mean you have to be a defeated Christian. You can still live a victorious life!

Isaiah 51:3 says, "For the Lord shall comfort Zion: he will comfort all her waste places." *As a Christian, you are part of the Church, a resident of spiritual Zion, but even in Zion, there will be* dry *times, and times when you feel wasted and used up. Do not lose hope! God will not leave you in the desert!* "And he will make her wilderness like Eden, and her desert like the garden of the Lord; joy and gladness shall be found therein, thanksgiving, and the voice of melody."

What a wonderful promise from a loving Father! Your waste places and your wildernesses will be visited by the Lord Himself—and turned into places of thanksgiving and melody.

Nehemiah describes the children of Israel during one of their most difficult times. They were both disillusioned and sad. They wept continuously and mourned because their burdens had overwhelmed them. Then, Nehemiah encouraged the people and said, "...*the joy of the Lord is your strength.*" (8:10).

The people probably said, 'Well, that's great for you, Nehemiah, but you don't know what we're going through." I made the mistake once of saying something like that to Jesus.

What a dumb thing to say to someone who experienced *more* pressure, pain, burdens than anyone ever has! Jesus faced adversity in its severest form—and conquered it at the cross. Because of what He did at Calvary, you can face your problems with confidence. Joy *can* replace fear!

Break the Chains

Sometimes struggles lead to bondage. If you are in chains today because of your burdens, you can do one of three things:
1. You can bury them.
2. You can battle them.
3. Or, you can break them.

There is a great song we used to sing in Bible school that says, "The Lion of Judah shall break every chain and give to us the victory again and again."

God says your burden will be taken away, from off your shoulders, from off your neck; it will be broken and destroyed because of the anointing. What can you do to break the chains of bondage in your life?

First, you must *identify* the things that are tearing you down. The Bible says you will know the truth, and the truth will set you free. Once you know the truth, you have to receive it as such—and then act on it.

Just because you have a Bible, does not mean you necessarily know how to live victoriously. Just because you listen to a sermon does not mean you are always walking in victory. Just because you are a Christian, does not mean you are living consistently as an overcomer. The fact is, you may be miserable.

Living victoriously means you understand what God says and you respond in obedience to it. I could say, "Here, eat this food; it will make you healthy and strong." And you could reply, "I know it is important to eat, and I realize I haven't eaten anything in a long time, but I am doing something else right now. I will eat some other time."

Knowing what you should do will not keep you from dying of starvation—you have to *act* on the truth!

Identify Lying Spirits

Nowhere is this more important than in the spirit realm, where the devil will try to convince you to believe his lies and deception.

A few years ago, I interviewed a young woman named Robyn Bunds. She is one of two women who had babies by cult leader David Koresh. Koresh named Robyn's baby Wisdom Day.

Robyn was raised in the Branch Davidian cult even before David

Koresh took charge. Her father was an engineer, yet he believed a lie. Her mother was a nurse, but she also believed a lie.

When Koresh took over, he brought with him a twisted interest in biblical prophecy. He said that God had given him three angels, or revelations, but he could not reveal them until their due season. He also claimed he had been given a "New Light," which enabled him to take other men's wives, and girls as young as twelve.

Koresh started studying Scriptures that talked about the Lamb who opened the seals in the book of Revelation. Eventually, he pieced together a hodgepodge teaching that gave him absolute authority over his followers, and which turned outsiders into "the enemy."

He called the first seal the New Light and said it referred to "the House of David," or, "the Seed of David." He said *his* seed was the seed of the Lamb that would establish the kingdom of God through the birth of Believers who would then rule the world. Before they could rule, Koresh's seed had to be received. He had to father the "children of God." Little girls in the Branch Davidians had a Star of David put around their necks when they reached the age of twelve, signifying their entrance to the House of David. They were to become the "brides of Christ," as Koresh put it. Robyn was one of those girls. She had no idea she was being deceived and seduced.

Robyn eventually left the cult and fought a bitter court battle for sole custody of her son. She won and later changed his name. I ministered to her for about three hours one day. I said, "Robyn, do you want to have peace?" Immediately, she started crying.

I prayed with her as she accepted Jesus Christ and urged her to burn the book that Koresh had given her with its perverted "Bible study" notes. Then, I sent her a new Bible and some things for her little boy, books with cassettes in them and other materials to help her.

Robyn's family believed a lie. The people in Waco's Branch Davidians believed a lie. They were good people, but a lying spirit deceived them.

Because they believed a lie, innocent people died. Babies died. Robyn's life was turned upside down by deception and trickery—until Jesus set things right.

When you believe a lie, a lying spirit takes control of your life. It causes you to make decisions that can devastate you and those you love. A lying spirit will prompt you to do things you later regret. It not only robs you of the victorious life Jesus intends for you to have, but cripples you emotionally, spiritually, mentally—even physically.

As a Christian, you have the God-given power and authority to reject the lies of the devil—*but you must know the truth of His Word and walk in obedience to it.* By saying "no" to lying spirits and "yes" to Jesus, you will find a renewed sense of joy.

Prioritize and Appraise

Once you have rediscovered your joy in the Lord, it is imperative that you maintain it, even in the midst of fear and turmoil. How? By reevaluating your priorities and accurately appraising the things that require your time and energy.

Let me say that again: examine the things you believe are important in your life, and ask God to help you prioritize them. Look at the way you spend your time and energy, and ask the Lord to help you determine what is valuable and what simply is "fluff." is Why is this so important? Because lying spirits will talk to you every day. They will try to steer you away from your God-given call with subtle and blatant deceptions. They will whisper in your ear, and you must be able to discern the truth of God from the lies of the devil. That is where prioritizing and appraising come in.

As a Christian, God wants you to treat His Word as a high priority. He wants you to appraise His Word as you would appraise a house, for instance, and assign a high value to it. His Word has *eternal* value, and it will not lead you astray.

When the devil tells you something, recognize it for what it is: a lie from the pit of hell. Do not dwell on it. Do not give it any time or attention. In other words, do not treat it as a high priority. Understand that the devil is never going to tell you anything valuable; he only has junk for sale. Your accurate appraisal of his lies can save you a lot of time and trouble—and help you replace fear and worry with faith and joy.

Let me give you an example. Television, magazines, movies, and billboards tell women that to be thin is to be attractive—the thinner the better. It does not matter if you are healthy—you should be thin as well. It does not matter if you are five feet two inches—you should still look like a runway model. You might be taller than most women; that does not matter either—you should still be thin. If you want to feel good about yourself, you have to be skinny.

Fashion is a fickle master, and it changes from one culture to the next. One year when my wife, Carolyn, and I were in Germany, we took a day trip to the Alps to see a famous castle. A king who thought women should be plump had ruled it; thin women were not at all appealing to him.

This king had three wives whom he called the three Graces, and he was so proud of them that he commissioned a special painting in their honor. He wanted the whole kingdom to see his lovely, rounded Graces.

Why am I telling you this story? Because it illustrates an important truth: if you determine your attitudes and responses by lies from the media, by advertisers who want to sell you something, and by carnal people who want you to be as defeated as they are, you will be crippled by fear and deception.

Jesus said the Holy Spirit would lead you into all truth. Pursue the truth of God and walk in it! Stop listening to lying spirits. Only then will you maintain the joy of the Lord.

The Wells of Salvation

Zephaniah 3:17 says, *"The Lord thy God in the midst of thee is mighty; he will save, he will rejoice over thee with joy; he will rest in His love, he will joy over thee with singing."* In Psalm 51:12, *David said, "Restore unto me the joy of thy salvation."* David was saying there is joy in salvation, that in the kingdom of God, there are no burden bearers with broken backs. God will not allow your burdens to break you or bury you if you appropriate His Word. Isaiah 12:2 says, *"Behold God is my salvation; I will trust, and not be afraid: for the Lord Jehovah is my strength and my song; he also is become my salvation. Therefore with joy shall ye draw water out of the wells of salvation."*

The Jewish people had a problem: The land was dry, and they needed water.

Whenever they moved to a new location, they did not start building houses, or buying goats, sheep, and cows. The first thing they did was look for water.

Finding water was more important than finding a house. It was more important than having children. It was their highest priority. If they did not find water, they had to dig a well. If they dug a well and it was dry, they had to move on and find another place to live. Once they found their well, they encountered another problem. Enemies would come with stones to block up the well, because they did not want the children of Israel in the land.

You may be experiencing a dry spell today. Perhaps you have been searching for water but have not found it yet. Or, maybe you have been besieged by spiritual enemies who have thwarted you at every turn. The Bible says, *"And with joy shall you draw water out of the wells of salvation"* (Isaiah 12:9).

If you are tired and thirsty, take heart! Jesus has invited you to come to Him and drink until you are filled to overflowing. He said He would give you living water that would flow from your innermost being!

The word for "salvation" in this Scripture is actually *"Yeshua,"* the Hebrew word for Jesus. With that in mind, you can read the scripture this way, *"With joy shall you draw water out of the wells of Jesus."* Think about it! Jesus will meet every need you have, whether you are weary, thirsty, under attack, or afraid of the future. He is your salvation! He is your joy!

Walk in the Spirit

If you want to have joy that overcomes your fear, understand that, in the natural, without God, it is impossible. If you want to live a *natural* life, simply go with the flow. Do what everyone else does. Watch the same movies, listen to the same music, and go to the same places. Do not make any decisions you might have to defend. Do not think about your relationships; just let them grow or flounder, as they will.

The only problem is that if you go with the flow, you will end up in the septic tank, for that is where the world's stream ultimately leads—to destruction. If you do not believe that, ask Jesus. You *must* make quality decisions. Right now, you may be facing a life-changing issue, and one thing is certain; when you are in the midst of change, everything seems equally important. Sometimes just sorting out the simplest things is exhausting. Should you take that new job? Can you afford to move? What will your family say? Can you leave your friends? How will you ever pay off your debts?

Confusion can cloud your perception and leave you vulnerable to fearful thinking. When this happens, you can respond in one of two ways: either back off and go with the flow, or rebuke the spirit of confusion, face your fears, and watch God move on your behalf.

You may think you cannot deal with your problems because they seem impossible—and in the natural, they are. With God, all things are possible! People told me I could not go and preach in the Kremlin.

"It is not possible," they said. They were right—it was not. No evangelist in America had ever walked into the Kremlin with a Bible, stood up, preached the gospel, and had an altar call. I was going in and attempting to do the impossible, in Jesus' name. I stood in the very spot where Communist leaders like Khrushchev and Brezhnev had vowed to bury us, where they cursed God, and I said, "Lenin is dead!" That statement had never been made in the Kremlin State Palace. No one would dare say "Lenin is dead," but I said it. I said, "Stalin is dead. Marx is dead. They have no power-—but Jesus of Nazareth is alive, and He is here to save your souls." I watched Russians by the thousands weave their way through the crowds to come and be saved. They came in as atheists but left as Christians, washed in the blood of the Lamb, holding Bibles under their arms and crying tears of joy. Nearly 7,000 Russians found Jesus that day. Hallelujah!

Finding Impossible Joy

What do you do when you are faced with an impossible situation?
1. Change your mind. Have you changed your clothes this week? Kind of important, isn't it, changing your clothes? Well, so is changing your mind.

   The Bible says to let peace rule your mind. The word *"rule"* here is Latin for "umpire." In other words, let the anointing of God be your umpire.

   Do not say, "I'll get everything under control. I can figure this out. I know what to do. Nobody needs to tell me." You must submit to the lordship of Jesus if you are to do the impossible and live an abundant life. Let peace be the umpire in your heart.
2. Go to the well of your salvation. Draw water out of the river of God. I know a wonderful song that says, "There is a river that flows from deep within." Go to that river. Go to the

Source of your supply: Jesus.

3. Cancel all debts. Debts are joy-stealers. If a person has hurt you, forgive him. If a person has sinned against you, stop feeling sorry for yourself.

   As my daughter, Rachel used to tell me, put a rubber band around your head and snap out of it. You will never succeed in life by having a pity party. No one wants to be around negative people; you lose friends as well as your peace and joy.

   Change your mind and stay at the well of your salvation. Remember that the Jews never built their homes, had children, or made any decisions until they found a well that could meet their needs. Make sure your well is flowing with living water, and keep drinking from it!

   Empty yourself of people who offend you. I had to empty myself at least 150 times in Russia. I had never met so many people who were determined to offend me. I realized God was in control, and the only way I was going to see Him do the impossible was if I trusted Him.

4. Do not give place to the devil. Another song that I used to sing says, "Joy is a flag flown high from the castle of my heart. The King is in residence there." Say to the demons of hell that the King is in residence in your life.

Bless the Lord

If you are burdened and do not feel any joy, what should you do? Start rejoicing. David brought a sacrifice of joy to God in the tabernacle. He said, *"Oh my soul, bless the Lord."* He did not sit around and meditate on his problems. He started thanking God for His goodness. Why not bless the Lord right now where you are? Thank Him for sharing your burden and replacing fear with joy. Receive His anointing—and praise Him for destroying the yoke.

CHAPTER TWENTY-TWO

Know Your Destiny

*God wants to give you a revelation in the Spirit
today—a revelation of destiny that will deliver you
from fear, inadequacy and compromise.*

America has become a spiritual desert, so we must make a straight highway in the desert for our God. Isaiah 40:3-5 says, *"The voice of him that crieth in the wilderness, Prepare ye the way of the Lord, make straight in the desert a highway for our God. Every valley shall be exalted, and every mountain and hill shall be made low: and the crooked shall be made straight, and the rough places plain: And the glory of the Lord shall be revealed, and all flesh shall see it together: for the mouth of the Lord hath spoken it."*

Isaiah makes the contrast between darkness and light. The point where darkness challenges light is the same point where God manifests His power and plan through man; it is the same point where He manifests His own glory!

Indeed, there are many points where darkness challenges the light of God. In America, we see it all around us. Lying, deceiving spirits, for example, manipulate much of what we see and hear in the media, as well as what we hear from many political and social leaders around the country.

Far too often, Americans have chosen to believe the spirits of deception and then walk in darkness. The result is rampant fear and confusion. Skepticism and unbelief overshadow the truth of God's Word. Dependence on Man replaces dependence on God.

It is hard to walk in faith when you are listening to news reports that say you could be robbed, mugged, raped, or murdered, and your children could turn to drugs, join a gang, or run away from home. It can be difficult to believe the truth when you are reading newspaper and magazine reports that focus on the growing crime rate and the demise of the family unit. It is, in fact, downright discouraging when you dwell on the problems around you, instead of meditating on Jesus, the problem solver!

When God is ignored, faith and vision die, and you become dependent on others. If you spend enough time filling your mind with God-less information, you will turn to Man to meet your needs when trouble comes. How many people are unable to cope with the pain and pressure of economic crisis, for instance, and so they turn to the federal government, or to state agencies for help? Without God, they become dependent on Man.

You may be a victim of disease. You may be discouraged and afraid. You may be up to your ears in debt. You may have lost your sense of direction in life. On the other hand, you may be struggling with a secret sin you cannot seem to conquer. You have a shortage. A shortage to God is merely an opportunity for Him to show you His faithfulness!

Darkness from God's Perspective

God sees darkness as a challenge. He does not see it as a time to retreat. God is light. He is eternal and cannot be overcome by any manifestation of darkness.

All through the Bible, God challenges the darkness to reveal His power, plan, and glory. For instance, Adam's life was dark and dismal when Cain murdered his younger brother Abel, but God gave Adam and Eve another son, Seth. Genesis 4:26 says, "And to Seth, to him also there was born a son; and he called his name Enos: then began men to call upon the name of the Lord." In the midst of darkness, God brought light and destiny.

Abraham's life was initially filled with the darkness of his father's idol worship, but God called Abraham out and revealed His power, plan, and glory to him. Abraham became the father of nations—and is called the Father of Faith. God challenged the darkness and led Abraham into the light of His destiny.

More Old Testament Examples

Jacob was called "the supplanter." He cheated his brother Esau out of his birthright and his father's blessing. For years, he struggled with the fear and darkness of his own heart—until he wrestled with the Lord one night. God challenged that darkness and changed not only Jacob's character but also his name. Jacob was transformed from being "the supplanter" to Israel, or "he who strives with God." That Divine challenge led to a covenant destiny that influenced the world.

Joseph was hated, despised, and slandered. His own brothers plotted his murder. He was sold into slavery, falsely accused of rape, and thrown into prison. In his darkest hour, God gave Joseph a wonderful gift; He gave him the ability to interpret dreams.

God challenged the darkness of unfair circumstances and revealed His destiny for a faithful servant. Joseph became Egypt's Prime Minister with two portfolios—the Secretary of State and Foreign Minister, and Senior Advisor at the same time!

Moses was a Hebrew whose life was spared when his mother set him adrift in a waterproof basket. Pharaoh's daughter found the baby in the Nile and raised him as her own. Moses became an idol worshipper like the Egyptians around him—until God challenged the darkness and released Moses to his true destiny as the deliverer of Israel.

Gideon was in deep depression, even despair, when God showed up with a mighty angel and called him a man of valor. In the midst of dark uncertainty, God challenged his discouragement and hopelessness—and replaced it with light, truth, and courage. In that moment, Gideon saw his true destiny, from God's perspective, and it changed his life.

David was the youngest of eight sons, a boy who wrote music and tended the sheep. He was brave enough to kill a lion and a bear with his own hands, but his family failed to see anything special about him.

When Samuel told Jesse that God had chosen one of his sons to be king, Jesse presented every one of his boys to the prophet—everyone but David. Finally, Samuel asked, "Are these all your children?" Jesse said his youngest son was in the field with the sheep. First Samuel 16:12 says, *"And he sent, and brought him in. Now he was ruddy, and withal of a beautiful countenance, and goodly to look to. And the Lord said, Arise, anoint him: for this is he."*

David was anointed King of Israel but he had to wait for several years before that destiny was realized. When the Philistines attacked Israel, they sent out a huge warrior named Goliath to taunt the troops. David's oldest brothers joined the army, but David had to stay at home and tend the sheep. One day, his father sent him to the battlefield with food for his brothers, but even then, David was mocked. Then, he heard of Goliath's threats. It was a dark time for the future King of Israel. God challenged the darkness once again! He brought courage to the heart of a faithful shepherd boy and enabled him to defeat the giant with a stone and slingshot.

Isaiah also faced the darkness. He was a negative, judgmental man. The book that bears his name begins with a series of gloomy pronouncements. "Woe unto them," he wrote repeatedly.

Then, in the midst of dark condemnation, Isaiah encountered the glory of the Lord—and his "woe unto them" attitude became a "woe is me" statement. God challenged his confidence and changed his life so radically that no other prophet had more revelations of the coming of the Messiah than Isaiah. He became a man of destiny whose words invited others to depend upon God, not Man.

An Example from the New Testament

Saul was a persecutor of the Church. He diligently tracked down Christians and made sure they were beaten, imprisoned, or put to death. He was a man of uncompromising zeal, but his zeal was misplaced. It was fanatic, dark—and dangerous.

One morning, Saul was on his way to Damascus when God challenged the darkness of his religious fervor. He was blinded by the light of God's Son and given a revelation that changed his life—and the destiny of the Church.

God healed Saul's heart and eyes, and changed his name to Paul. Indeed, God took a misguided zealot and filled him with the glory of Jesus. He revealed to Paul his true destiny—as an apostle, teacher, and missionary to the Gentiles, whose letters now comprise two-thirds of the New Testament!

How Do You Respond?

The men and women of the Bible were not overcomers because they never had problems. No! They overcame their fear, their circumstances, and their prejudices by trusting God and by receiving His Word. They discovered their destiny in the midst of darkness. Their suffering strengthened their faith and deepened their dependence on God.

How do you respond to the dark times in your life? Do you face the darkness as a soldier in God's victorious army, as an overcomer? Do you face the darkness with a tender and repentant heart? Or, do you retreat from the darkness? Does pressure expose your anger and unbelief? When darkness threatens to overtake you, do you lash out at God and others? Do dark moments make you want to compromise your faith?

The devil will do whatever he can to keep you from seeing your own sin. He will try to blind you with fear and unbelief. He will deceive you and bring confusion into every area of your life. He wants you to play the Blame Game! He wants you to judge others! He wants you to make excuses for your sin!

The devil wants to steal your joy and render you ineffective. When you allow the darkness to overtake you, you grieve the Holy Spirit and nullify the Word of Truth in your life, making you vulnerable to further deception and defeat.

When you refuse to stand against darkness in the name of the Lord, three things happen:

1. Your appropriation of God's righteousness is impeded.
2. Your vision of Jesus is dimmed and distorted.
3. Your strength and ability to overcome the darkness fail.

You Can Overcome!

What can you do to overcome darkness in your life?

1. Cancel all debts. Do not hold onto debts of bitterness, unforgiveness, deception, or secret sin. Go to the cross of Christ and cancel all your debts! Confess your sin, especially the dark, secret sins that have held you in bondage. Let Jesus wash you in His blood! You can be clean!

    You do not have to carry bitterness and unforgiveness any longer! You can let go of your anger! You do not have to play the Blame Game! You can receive truth, and walk in real, lasting liberty. You do not have to live with guilt, condemnation, or defeat!

2. Empty yourself of pride and every preconceived idea that does not line up with the Word of God. Get rid of all your carnal thoughts. Stop relying on your head knowledge, and start relying on Jesus.

   Let the Spirit of God lead you! Stop depending on your education, your intuition, temperament, emotions, or other people. Empty yourself daily and ask God to fill you with His Spirit— and reveal His destiny for your life.

3. Take responsibility for your own actions. Deal with your unbelief, fear, and anger. Admit them all to God.

   Do not allow yourself to be deceived. Don't allow pride to keep you from experiencing God's blessing!

4. Follow your favor. Know what God has called *you* to do, then do it. Do not copy other Christians or ministries—unless you are following their example of love and faithfulness.

   Ask God to show you what He is blessing in your life. Then, ask Him to show you specifically how He wants you to bless others.

5. Invest in people. Make up your mind that the most precious resource in your life is not your money, your job, your house, or your car. God does not care about things. He cares about people. So should you!

   Make a list of godly people who encourage you and who speak the Word of Christ. Make those people part of your life and invest in them. Love them. Pray for them. Spend time with them. Build them up in the Lord.

This Is Your Day of Destiny!

You do not have to let fear and darkness control your life any longer. This is your day of destiny! It does not have to be a time of defeat and discouragement. Romans 8:19 says, "*For the earnest expectation of the creature waiteth for the manifestation of the sons of God.*"

Do not fill your mind with reports of gloom and doom. Listen to what God says. God wants to give you a revelation in the Spirit today—a revelation of destiny that will deliver you from fear, inadequacy and compromise.

If you will allow the Lord to speak to your heart, you will not be swayed by the fear, skepticism, confusion and anger so prevalent in our society today. You will not be overcome by darkness. Instead, you will walk in truth and light.

Darkness never overpowers the light of God. God challenges the darkness and reveals His will in the midst of the struggle. There, you will discover your destiny—and that revelation will change your life.

CHAPTER TWENTY-THREE

Let His Glory Fill the Temple

*When you are hungry for the Spirit, God won't give
you just a little—He will give you all He has and
everything He has is in Jesus.*

Are you hungry for the righteousness of God? If so, you must learn to let God do what He wants to do—and what He wants to do is manifest His glory in you! Aren't you tired of deadness? Haven't you had enough of fear and worry? Don't you want faith and joy to fill your heart? Aren't you ready for change? Then, why not let the Holy Spirit take control?

Glory in Your Temple

Jesus said, *"For where two or three are gathered together in my name, there am I in the midst of them."* (Matthew 18:20). Whenever you meet together with other Believers to honor the Lord, He is there with you. The Holy Ghost is there to impart the glory of God to you. Angels are present to minister to you. There, in the midst of praise and worship, is an atmosphere of hope and expectation. Faith is strengthened and anointing released.

When Solomon dedicated the temple, the glory of the Lord came in such majesty that it filled the entire place, and priests could not continue their work! Second Chronicles 5:13-14 declares, *"It came even to pass, as the trumpeters and singers were as one, to make one sound to be heard in praising and thanking the Lord; and when they lifted up their voice with the trumpets and cymbals and instruments of music, and praised the Lord, saying, For he is good; for his mercy endureth for ever: that then the house was filled with a cloud, even the house of the Lord; So that the priests could not stand to minister by reason of the cloud: for the glory of the Lord had filled the house of God."*

The temple Solomon built was beautiful, but it cannot begin to compare with your heart. From the beginning, God intended to dwell in a "house not made of stones." His desire was to live in you and fill you with His glory! First Corinthians 6:19-20 says, *"What? know ye not that your body is the temple of the Holy Ghost which is in you, which ye have of God, and ye are not your own? For ye are bought with a price: therefore glorify God in your body, and in your spirit, which are God's."*

When God fills your temple, or your heart, His glory is manifested. You exhibit peace and joy, love, fruitfulness, compassion for the lost, and kindness toward the poor. You nurture the fatherless and the widows. You serve with a heart of tenderness. God's anointing is evident as you step out in faith to bring salvation, healing, and deliverance to those in need.

Across this nation and around the world, God is touching the hearts of men and women who yearn for intimacy with Him. He is nourishing those who are hungry for righteousness, for He is the Bread of Life.

"Re-Filled" with the Spirit

You need His glory to fill your temple, just as you need His anointing. You need to be filled with the Spirit—daily! Ephesians 5:18 says, *"And be not drunk with wine, wherein is excess; but be filled with the Spirit;"* That verse actually means, "be continually filled." Do not just ask for the infilling and then stop! Ask the Holy Ghost to fill you with His power and anointing every day so you can do the will of God.

You may already have the gift of tongues, and that is good. You may have the gift of prophecy or miracles. Praise God! But don't count on the gifts alone to deepen your relationship with Jesus. You must be filled again and again—because you need more and more of Jesus!

I know I need more of Jesus today than I did yesterday. That is because I am changing and growing. My needs and expectations are changing. My understanding is maturing. The same is true for you!

As your faith grows, so does your responsibility. Your intercession for others needs to grow. Your study of the Word needs to grow. And for that, you need more of Jesus.

When you are hungry for the Spirit, God will not just give you a little—He will give you all He has, and everything He has is in Jesus.

Glory or Gone Fishing?

When you are spiritually hungry, you are not satisfied with cold, lifeless sermons. You are not content with Christian social clubs. You do not want to keep hearing "the same old same old" repeatedly.

You want to be taught how to stand on the Word of God. You want to be challenged to walk in faith. You want to be stirred out of your complacency, so you can fulfill your destiny in Jesus. You want to be confronted—then, you want to know you are loved.

If the glory of God is not present in your life, you might as well hang a sign around your neck that reads, "Gone Fishing." There won't be anything else to do. Your life will just be a series of events without the vision, power, and direction of the Holy Ghost.

Are you hungry for more? Do you yearn for the touch of God? If so, get ready! The Lord is on His way, and when Jesus shows up, all of your impossible missions become "mission possible."

God does not want to be limited by your schedule or your preferences. You cannot tell Him what to do in your life, or how to do it. You just submit yourself, and let Him be God.

One Big Jesus

It is important that you have the right attitude as you seek the Lord. James 4:6-8, 10 says, *"But he giveth more grace. Wherefore he saith, God resisteth the proud, but giveth grace unto the humble. Submit yourselves therefore to God. Resist the devil, and he will flee from you. Draw nigh to God, and he will draw nigh to you...Humble yourselves in the sight of the Lord, and he shall lift you up."*

God expects you to walk humbly before Him. There are no big guys in the kingdom of God; there is just one big Jesus. If you love Him, you will want to serve Him. You will say, "Father, Thy will be done in my life. Fill me with Your glory so that Jesus is magnified in me."

Pray that God will breathe life into your weary soul. Ask Him to reveal Himself to you. Then, thank Him for all that He has done in your life. As you begin to praise and worship Him, your faith will be ignited, and you will *know* He is alive and at work in *you.*

God wants to take your hungry, aching heart, and fill it with His Spirit!

Caught Up in His Glory

Mary Woodsworther was so filled with the Holy Ghost that she started preaching in St. Louis one night. The power of God hit her, and she became so caught up in the Spirit that she froze like an icicle right in the middle of her sermon.

For two days, she could not move. She was like a statue. One hundred and twenty thousand people poured into St. Louis to see this woman who did not blink an eye, nor move a muscle for 48 hours under the power and the glory of God. Newspapers everywhere wrote about it.

When the glory of God was lifted, she never missed a sentence. She continued her sermon exactly where she left off 48 hours before. She was caught up in the glory.

John Knox of Scotland also experienced the glory of God. I went to Scotland once with a brother, and we were part of a glorious move of God.

People told us, "You can't have revival in Scotland; it's spiritually dry and emotionally cold."

But we didn't listen to them. We *knew* God was going to touch people, and that was enough for us. We began the services, and indeed, the power of God fell. It was so strong one night that nobody left the place walking. They were being dragged out because of the glory—they didn't know what hit them. They were praying and, suddenly, Jesus showed up. God will always show up for those who want His glory.

A Change in Theology

John Wesley was a dynamic Methodist preacher who loved God but did not understand the workings of the Holy Ghost. One night, the glory was so strong that a woman fell to the floor during one of his meetings, slain under the power of God. She broke out in holy laughter, and when he tried to quiet her, she laughed at him.

Forty-five minutes later, Wesley changed his theology. He realized the woman was not manufacturing anything. She certainly did not intend to put on a show. He realized he was in the midst of a glorious move of God, and he submitted himself to it. That experience changed Wesley's life and ministry.

William Seymour was the founder of an organization called The Evening Light Saints. He was a precious black man who could see with only one eye. He spent his life preaching in bars, barns, and little shanty towns—until he came to a thoroughfare called Azusa Street. The lectern from which he preached consisted of two large, square wooden boxes. Until moved by the Spirit to speak, Rev. Seymour would sit on a chair behind the pulpit. Deep in prayer, he would plunge his head into the top box while waiting for the Lord to speak through him.

That move of God shook America to its roots. As a result of Seymour's faithfulness, millions of souls have been filled with the Holy Spirit throughout the world since the days of Azusa Street. You must come out of your comfort zone. When you do, you will look at the problems you face from your position in Jesus. When you get out of your comfort zone, God will get hold of you, and suddenly, you will connect with the Holy Spirit.

Moving in God's Dimension

The Word says you must run with perseverance the race that is set before you. When you move in God's dimension, you set all other things aside. The natural man does not understand this. The natural man is trying to win the rat race. The only problem with trying to win the rat race is that there will always be a rat that runs faster than you do. You cannot outrun the rats!

But as a Christian, you don't have to. All you have to do is submit to the work of the Holy Ghost and move when Jesus says, "Move." When the Holy Ghost touches you, you will be filled with His glory.

It will put joy and supernatural power in your life. You will rise above your circumstances. You will take authority over fear, worry, doubt, sickness, and sin. No matter how the devil tries to tempt you, you will stand firm in the power of the Holy Ghost.

Hungry for His Glory

As God fills you with His glory, His anointing is also released. When you empty yourself and acknowledge the lordship of Jesus, God will begin to take control of every area of your life. When I first submitted myself to the work of the Holy Ghost, I felt God's joy come upon me. It just bubbled up from within. I hadn't had a really good belly laugh in a long time, but it broke out in me, and I just couldn't control it.

The Bible says the Spirit of God demonstrates Himself. The disciples saw that in Jesus, and it ruined them for any other way of life. That is why they tarried at Pentecost. When they saw the glory on Jesus, it provoked them to say, "Lord, what must we do? Father, let your glory fall." You will get a touch from God when you seek Him with all your heart. God will not shortchange you! He loves you and is a kind, generous Father! Reach out to Him right now. He wants to fill your temple with His glorious Holy Spirit.

CHAPTER TWENTY-FOUR

Realize the Best is Yet to Come

The blood of Jesus cries out to the Church, saying,
"The hour is late. The best is yet to come."

God has blessed you in a marvelous way! He has given you a living hope! Be encouraged today! You do not have to live with fear! You are an overcomer! Second Peter 3:5 says, *"Blessed be the God and Father of our Lord Jesus Christ, which according to His abundant mercy hath begotten us again to a lively hope by the resurrection of Jesus Christ from the dead, To an inheritance incorruptible, and undefiled, and that fadeth not away, reserved in heaven for you, Who are kept by the power of God through faith unto salvation ready to be revealed in the last time."*

The world does not understand this truth. They look at Christians and think we are foolish. They laugh at us. They say to themselves, "You won't do anything of real significance. You can't succeed unless you do what we do. You must compromise and play our game." But they are so very wrong.

Fulfilling the Promise

I believe the best God has for you is yet to come. Let me give you some reasons why:

1. The best is yet to come because of His *promises.* As a Christian, you have been given great and glorious promises, none of which have faded away or changed.

    Jesus conquered death, and no one has taken the keys away from Him! That is why the Bible says if you walk through the valley of the shadow of death, you should fear no evil.

    When my son was young, he was fascinated with shadows. When he looked at a shadow, he would ask, "What's that?"

    "It's you," I answered.

    "Look how big I am," he replied.

    The shadow is a reflection of the object. The scripture says when you walk through the valley of the shadow of death, you are walking through its reflection, its image. Death has lost its sting. For the Believer, all that is left is a shadow. No fear remains.

    You have a great promise—Jesus Christ will return to earth one day soon! Glory to God! The King of kings is on His way! The Lord of lords is coming! Philippians 2:10 says, "That at the name of Jesus every knee should bow, of things in heaven, and things in earth, and things under the earth; And that every tongue should confess that Jesus Christ is Lord, to the glory of God the Father."

    The nature and character of Jesus is depicted throughout the Scriptures in dramatic types and shadows: He is still Gideon's mighty Man of valor, still Jacob's Israel, still Joseph's Prime Minister, still Moses' Deliverer, still the Bread of Life, still the Good Shepherd, still the Rose of Sharon.

    The promise has not changed. When you need salvation, deliverance, healing, and anointing, go to Jesus. He is still the Water of Life, the Lion of Judah, and the Rock of Ages. That is why the best is yet to come!

The demons of hell cannot continue to hold you captive if you are trusting Jesus to set you free! Satan has been defeated. Jesus is the victor, and He reigns in you!

2. The best is yet to come because of HIS prophetic return. Jesus has not forgotten you. He is coming back for His Bride. Ephesians 5:27 says, *"That he might present it to himself a glorious church not having spot, or wrinkle, or any such thing; but that it should be holy and without blemish."*

   In the interim, He is teaching His people to walk in love and holiness. He is also getting "the house" ready for His Bride. In John 14:2, He said, *"In my Father's house are many mansions...I go to prepare a place for you."* One translation of the Bible says He is preparing "many positions."

   Think of it! Not only will Jesus give you an eternal home, but a position! You will have rank and authority. But that's not all! In Acts 3:19-20, Peter talks about the outpouring of the Holy Spirit, *"Repent ye therefore, and be converted, that your sins may be blotted out, when the times of refreshing shall come from the presence of the Lord; And he shall send Jesus Christ, which before was preached unto you."*

   Peter is prophesying of an outpouring of the Holy Spirit, which is to come! That outpouring will cause the Jews to repent and come to Jesus by the tens of thousands! Get ready! The Spirit of God is moving, and Jesus is on His way!

3. The best is yet to come because there is *preparation* to be made. Jesus is in favor of preparation and strategy. One of the simplest, yet vital, truths you can ever realize is that God is smarter than you are.

   In John 14:12, Jesus said, *"Greater works than these shall he do; because I go to the Father..."* That is preparation.

Jesus is saying, "I will bring national revival, world deliverance, the salvation of the lost, and the mighty outpouring of the Holy Ghost. I will do great and mighty things, but I will do them through you. As you go in My name, be confident, and know that I am with you. Believe that you will do greater things than I did when I walked the earth, because I have sent the Holy Ghost to live in you and lead you in the way you should go. I will not leave you. I shed My own holy blood to protect you and bring you into the family of God. Now, I am interceding for you. Rejoice, and go in peace!"

4. The best is yet to come because of your *position* in Him. Jesus will not return for a bunch of losers. He will take those who know they are His; they know they are *in* Him, just as He is in them—and both Jesus and His followers are in the Father. In John 17:21, Jesus prayed, *"That they all may be one; as thou; Father, art in me, and I in thee, that they also may be one in us: that the world may believe that thou has sent me."*

Verse 22 says, *"And the glory which thou gavest me I have given them; that they may be one, even as we are one."* Jesus has given you His power and glory so that the world would believe He is the only begotten Son of God!

When my son was four years old, he told me, "God has called me into the ministry. I will have to work hard because you do, Dad."

"Mikey," I replied, "you are smarter than I am. You might even be a genius."

"Dad, I don't need to be a genius, because Jesus is in me and He is a genius!" he said.

There has never been a problem that Jesus could not solve. The same still holds true for you! Jesus is in you, and you are in Him.

Together, you can overcome fear, worry, poverty, anger, and unbelief!

5. The best is yet to come because of the *purchase price*. How much did Jesus pay for you? How much did it cost Him to redeem you? Was His blood powerful enough?

   Why was the veil in the holy of holies torn in two as the blood of Jesus flowed from His hands, His feet, and His side? Why did the ground open up, allowing the dead to rise when His blood was shed? Why did the sky turn dark when Jesus died? Why was there so much glory on Jesus?

   Because the blood of Jesus is the most powerful force in the universe! But listen, Christian, the hour is late. There is no time for compromise. Stand up! Be healed in the name of Jesus! Declare His Word! The best is yet to come!

6. The best is yet to come because of the program. The gospel of Jesus Christ shall be preached in all the earth—and then He is coming back.

   You have a God who looks into the wilderness, the deserts, and wastelands. He sees your dry heart. He sees your barren life. He sees your empty soul. And in that place of death and despair, He brings life and renewal, "streams in the desert" to refresh and restore.

   China has the largest population in the world. Several years ago, students marched in Tiananmen Square and cried out for freedom. Change is coming. Why? So there is liberty to preach the gospel of Jesus Christ!

   The doors are opening all around the world: in China, Africa, Russia, and countless other nations—to preach the gospel and set the captives free!

7. The best is yet to come because Jesus is *praying* and interceding for you—for the lost and hurting, for God's people and for His leaders who are equipping the saints to minister in

His name.

You may be tired of the daily struggle, but if you will allow the Holy Ghost to revive your spirit and soul, your mind and body, and your strength, then you will find you have fresh dreams, new revelations, and a continuous release of the anointing in your life.

Pray for wisdom. Pray for direction. Pray in Jesus' name and expect answers to come!

A Holy People

The world does not know what it needs today—but you do. You can meet that need with boldness and grace, in the name of Jesus.

Ephesians 1:3 says, *"Blessed be the God and Father of our Lord Jesus Christ, who hath blessed us with all spiritual blessings in heavenly places in Christ."*

You are part of a great and wonderful family, a holy and royal people in Christ Jesus. You are a soldier in the army of God. You are called, anointed, filled, blessed, and equipped. You are *more* than a conqueror in Him.

Take courage as you go in His name, and remember, the best is yet to come!